DEANO

From Gipsyville to the Premiership

Dean Windass

With Simon Parker

**TO MY FAMILY,
MY WIFE AND MY KIDS**

Simon Parker, who is married with three children, reports on Bradford City for the Bradford Telegraph & Argus. He is grateful to Dean for supplying an endless list of back pages down the years.

Great Northern Books
PO Box 213, Ilkley, LS29 9WS
www.greatnorthernbooks.co.uk

First published 2007
New edition in paperback 2008
© Dean Windass and Simon Parker 2007, 2008

ISBN: 978 1 905080 49 6

Design and layout: David Burrill

Cover Photography: Jack Harland, Hull Daily Mail

Printed in Great Britain by Clays Ltd, St Ives plc

CIP Data
A catalogue for this book is available from the British Library

CONTENTS

FOREWORD

BY PHIL BROWN

A LOT OF MANAGERS around this level would be a little bit frightened of signing the likes of Dean Windass. Like Nick Barmby, he's a son of Hull; a Hull City fan man and boy. One of their own. Every fan wants him to come back to his hometown club. It sounds like the perfect signing.

But some managers might fear that he will be too big a presence; that maybe he could be a threat to their job. You've got an experienced player who wants to get into management one day, and you're bringing him back to the club where he is idolised.

But management is not that easy. Chances don't come along just because you've got an affinity with the football club.

In an awful lot of instances in the game, it's a case of being in the right place at the right time. And it takes time to climb the coaching ladder.

I never once worried about Deano being at the club again. I was fully confident in my own ability as a manager and as I felt he was the right man for our team then it was a no brainer.

Having met the lad, his wife and family on holiday a few times, I knew he was a character. And when I sat down with him to talk properly, I could see his desire to play for the club again.

Meeting a player is so important because you can tell what he really thinks. And looking into the whites of his eyes, I could see that ambition still burning fiercely.

His body language told me everything. He couldn't wait to come aboard.

We needed a goal scorer desperately when Dean came in. We were at the wrong end of the Championship and our top scorer at the time was Jon Parkin on six. Outside of that we had a couple of fives and fours.

We lacked that double-figure man and Dean fitted the bill. He had already got that many for Bradford so I knew what he was capable of.

And with Dean, we weren't just signing a very experienced striker but also a capable midfield player with a great eye for a pass. He was a fantastic acquisition in our position.

Some might have said it was a risk but I saw it as a calculated risk. He was fit and hungry and confident of playing well again at a higher level.

And Dean being Dean made sure everyone knew about it. He decided to shout it from the rooftops that he had come back to save Hull City from relegation.

Not one to hold back, he went out and told the world that he would score the goals to keep us up.

That impressed me. It was a sign of courage.

Here was a player who wasn't afraid to back his own ability. He talked the talk because he was good enough to walk the walk.

Dean wanted the number nine shirt which brings with it a sense of expectation. That just spurred him on more.

He is the type of player who will look in the mirror after every game and ask himself "did I do a good job out there or could I have done any better?"

That's the sort of person I want in my dressing room. As far as I'm concerned, I want a strong body of men to play for my football club not a bunch of weaklings that will wilt under pressure.

The kids can learn from having the likes of Deano around. I want them to be able to survive in that environment and grow stronger because of it.

Dean is old school. As an apprentice, he had to knock on the door and wait. Football may have moved on since then, certainly management has, but I believe that you still need to instil that discipline.

He loves the game and he is deadly serious about it. Now Dean is saying that he is going to play on until he is 45 and you wouldn't bet against him doing that.

Of course I was conscious of the fact that we were signing a 38-year-old. But I was also conscious that he had never been quick so it was not a case of him losing that element of speed over the years.

That isn't his game. We've got pace elsewhere in the team; pace alongside Dean Windass. All he needs to do is focus on being in the right place at the right time - something he has done through all of his career.

I admit I treat Dean differently from some of the younger players. But I have always done that with the elder statesmen. They deserve being treated with the utmost respect and so do their bodies.

We had a lot of players at Bolton who came in during their 30s at a time when people maybe thought their best days were over. People like Youri Djorkaeff and Fernando Hierro had a great attitude towards hard work and wanted to play and train all the time, just like Dean.

It's one of my hardest jobs to stop them from time to time and force them to take that extra day off, even if they don't want to. The less they do on the training ground, the more they can do on the field in matches.

Dean just wants to be out there on the training ground every day. That's what he has done for nearly 20 years.

He's got a great attitude in training and will always give it his all.

He hates missing a session but there are occasions when I have to force him to stay away and rest.

He needed a rest after we played QPR last season. Then I put him on the bench for the next game at Barnsley which was on Sky.

He came on and scored with his first touch after 30 seconds - that's a typical response!

I personally never doubted that he would do the business for us again. I had to improve our strike force and his partnership with young Fraizer Campbell from Manchester United has been superb.

We needed one double-figure man to get into the top half of the table. With two, I knew we could make the play-offs.

And it was just written in the stars that Dean should get our winning goal at Wembley. A fantastic strike to seal a fantastic season.

Dean's new contract was never in doubt. He isn't winging it at all. He fully deserves the new deal for the way he performs every time he crosses that white line.

He will be 40 before the end of next season but, as Dean says, age is just a number. I've no qualms about him still playing five years from now.

FOREWORD

BY BRYAN ROBSON

DEANO isn't exactly the kind of lad you forget in a hurry. He likes to be the centre of attention, enjoying the banter on the field or in the dressing room. Despite the larking about though, he has a work ethic that many others would do well to copy.

The first time he really caught my eye was when I took my then Middlesbrough side down to Valley Parade for a third round FA Cup match against Bradford City early in 2001. We won the game, but Deano stole the show and I soon tabled a bid to bring him to the Riverside.

At that time, Terry Venables was working alongside me during a difficult spell at the club. We were threatened with relegation and needed all hands on deck to avoid dropping out of the Premiership. Dean came in, settled well and instantly got on with the other lads. He gave us a boost on and off the field and played his part in keeping the club in the top flight.

Dean's goals and mischievous sense of humour also won over the fans and he was a popular figure on Teesside (a figure that's also amused opposition fans over the years).

Myself and Deano worked together for a second time at Bradford and his attitude was still the same, always asking questions of himself, striving to be the very best player he can be. The work ethic that got him to the top has prolonged his professional career. He's still banging in the goals now when other players he started out with have long since hung up their boots.

The simple reason for this longevity is his love of the game. Deano is one of the few who would genuinely turn up every Saturday and play for no pay. That's why the supporters, wherever he's been, have warmed to him and understood him. They see him as one of their own.

Clowning around and playing to the crowd is in his nature, but in the time I worked with him, he was never late for training, and whatever I asked him to do in training, he worked hard at.

I believe he is an under-rated player. His goal scoring record across his career stands up alongside the best. He's scored goals in every competition he's played in and his goals to games ratio is very good – despite the fact he's played in midfield for much of his career (against his wishes of course).

I know he's been doing his coaching badges and is looking to get into management when his time on the field comes to an end. He may well surprise a few people who have all too quickly written him off as a 'daft' bloke who doesn't take his football seriously enough.

Dean's always listened and learned from whoever's managed him at his respective clubs. Inevitably he's watched and taken note when mistakes have been made, and he will also have gained plenty of knowledge.

From my own personal point of view, it was a pleasure working with Deano and I look forward to our paths crossing again.

SATURDAY
MAY 24, 2008.
3.38PM.

Campbell just outside the D. Faced by Fontaine. Ghosts past him. A second defender. Goes past him.

Held up there. Chips it back to Windass edge of the area. There's the volley ....

Dean Windass has scored at Wembley for Hull City! A fantastic volley!

Dare we say it's a Wembley Windass winner!

What a goal from the 39-year-old. A Hull boy.

Even at 39 he is still a boy. What a Wembley finish that is!

DAVID BURNS, BBC Radio Humberside.

The goal. The f******* goal. I could cry just talking about it now. I've got that bit of commentary on my mobile. It sets me off every time I hear the words. The whole thing is etched on my brain. Shut my eyes and that ball goes flying into the Bristol City net. Every f******* time.

I started the move by nodding the ball out to Nicky Barmby, who had a touch then took it on. Fraizer made one run and then a second down the left hand side. He burst into the box and took three Bristol City defenders with him, Carey slipping over just as he was

about to tackle him. Nicky had gone to the back stick so I decided there was no point

in me running in there with him. And anyway, Fraizer couldn't cross it because of the defenders around him. The ball would have got blocked.

So instead I stood still and hung back on the edge of the penalty area, hoping that Fraizer might pick me out. He had to check as he reached the line and then looked up and

dinked the ball back to me. For a young boy to do that on such a big stage shows a hell of a lot of composure. As he chipped the pass up, I thought there was somebody behind me. I expected the left back to have tracked back and if I took a touch, it would give him the time to launch a tackle. So I just hit it ...

Like any golfer will tell you, you know when the ball has hit the sweet spot. Just pick your tee up and walk away, thank you very much. As soon as I connected, I f******* knew that ball was going in. Pick that one out.

And when it hit the net .... oh my God! That split-second will never sink in until the day I die. It will live with me forever. You score a goal like that at the most famous football stadium in the world for your hometown club to go up into the Premier League for the first time! Eighty-six thousand crowd all off their feet. It is what dreams are made of. A f******* fairytale? No, it's better than that.

I told you I'd do it, gaffer!

FAT BOY'S BACK

EIGHT POUNDS. Get in there. Once again, they won't be taking any money from the Windass pocket. It's the first day of pre-season and we're all put on the scales. It's the moment of truth - a pound for every pound over the weight you finished last year. No worries about that on my account. Check the figure from May and look at the new one - eight pounds lower. That will keep the other lads on their toes. Not bad for a fat bastard, eh! But no doubt I'll still take the stick from opposition fans next season, I always do. I'll have to be anorexic before they shut up but it doesn't bother me.

I'm used to it, just like pre-season. I've nearly done 20 of them now and it doesn't get any easier. Some lads really hate this time of the year but I don't mind. I love the craic and having a bit of banter seeing everyone again. Of course it's going to be hard, it's meant to be, but hard work never hurt anyone.

The first day is always fairly straightforward. You have a gentle run, 20 minutes or so, just to get people into it and then gradually build things up from there. The methods have changed over the years and players appreciate that. A few years back, you wouldn't see a ball for ages. It was just running, running, bloody running. Now most managers try to combine both and get the training games in early which is how it should be. You can do as much running as you like and when it comes to games, you're still blowing a bit.

Doing the long runs, I know I'll be near the front. That must piss off the younger lads - I know I wouldn't like getting beat by someone 20 years older. The funny thing is I couldn't really do it as a young kid. They'd all be finished and stood around waiting for me to catch up which was really embarrassing. I'd be sent off on my run first, 30 seconds before the rest, and still come in last. How humiliating is that!

But I worked at it over the years, I had to. And now for the last five years I've been at the front, maybe even longer than that. You get some of the stragglers shouting "slow down, slow down". Then when it comes to the 100m all the quick lads disappear in the distance. You don't see them slowing down for me, just their arses heading off in the dust.

I'm a strong runner but no manager has ever signed me for my pace. Mind you, they say the same about Teddy Sheringham and he hasn't done too badly for himself. The gaffer knows I won't just run down the channels like some of the younger, quicker strikers but as you get older you choose when to make the right runs at the right times. The first couple of yards are in the head, see the opportunity before the defender and react first. If you're clever, you learn the diagonal runs, to suck people into the ball. That's what I've done the last few years.

So I'm no sprinter but the longer distances suit me fine. I do them all the time. Even on holiday, I'll make sure the hotel has got a gym where I can do 20 to 25 minutes on the treadmill. It also helps that my wife Helen is a runner so over the years we've gone out training together on the roads. It always helps to keep you going when you've got company. But a lot of it is mental. You always get the whingers and whiners in the squad complaining but they still do it. They think they can't go any further but they still manage. There are no excuses for quitting; it's the same with anything.

I always try to come back very healthy for pre-season. You need that head start especially as the years tick away. But I've never let myself go during the summer. Funnily enough, I'd rather have a drink during the season than out of it. Typical awkward bugger doing things backwards. I'm feeling really good this year because I haven't touched a drink for a month. I swear to you, a drop of alcohol has not passed these lips. And it has made a difference. So much for the fat bastard.

It sounds a bit strange but the part of pre-season that I don't really like is the games. Don't get me wrong, I love playing football but it's just the friendlies that I don't enjoy. Whatever anyone says, they're not proper games. You can't get really involved and tackle like you'd want to because nobody wants to get injured. It must be a nightmare for defenders because they have to get stuck in and make last-ditch challenges to save a goal otherwise they get slaughtered. They can't jump out the way.

But I'm more worried about getting hurt and missing the first game of the season which is why I always have a word with the defenders I'm playing against. I just ask them to go steady. I won't go to elbow you if you promise not to try and tackle me too hard. There's no point in people kicking you and everyone getting frustrated in a game that's only there to improve your fitness.

It's all about building up to the opening fixture when it does matter. It would be stupid to miss that just because you've been a bit of a hero in a pointless friendly. And who cares if you win or lose? Some people get worked up if the pre-season results are crap but I've been in teams who haven't won a friendly and then gone unbeaten in the first month of the season.

Pre-season friendlies are just a guide - or an excuse for fans to have a few beers in the sun. If I was a punter I wouldn't bother to go along and I'd love to hear the views of the supporters who do. What makes them turn up? It's pretty obvious that nobody is playing at their 100 per cent maximum because it's early doors and the players don't want to get kicked or injured. I'll jump out of tackles as well as making a few silly runs just to keep building the fitness levels.

That's why I prefer to play against Premier League teams because they are all thinking the same. Nobody really gives a toss about the score. The problems come against non-league ones who are all going out to gub you. They'd love to be in your shoes and want to make a point. They are trying to put one over the bigger club so the result really matters to them. I suppose it doesn't look too bad for the fans after a few pints and a pie. The weather is good and you can watch the local team again but you still won't persuade me. Bring on the real deal. Then try holding me back.

AWAY DAY

IT'S FRIDAY AFTERNOON, 2pm, and the weekend starts here. We've had a light training session and lunch – chicken as always – and now it's time to get on the bus.

The traveling is a real drag but it's part of your job in football. You get on the coach every other week for an away game, go up and down the same motorways, going the same speed, seeing the same places. This is the part of the game that nobody sees and it can drive you mad. You have to come up with ways to pass the time.

Some lads are lucky enough to be able to sleep all the way. I've known team-mates who can kip on a clothes line. As soon as the engine starts up they are off to the land of nod.

The younger ones watch their DVDs or get on the Playstation. I play cards or listen to a few tunes on my iPod.

There are a couple of card schools at Bradford and I'm in the clever one near the front. There's usually me, Redders the physio, Marc Bridge-Wilkinson and Russell Howarth.

Russ, our reserve keeper, is a great player – at cards. He normally wins most of the hands. We play hearts and have a few quid on it but nothing major. We're not talking the England gamblers here. It's just for the fun of it and the chance to wind up the others. But mainly to help another boring journey pass a little bit quicker.

When the cards are finished, I might stick on the headphones. The other lads cane me for my taste in music and never let me put it on the speakers. I'm into all sorts from the sixties, seventies and eighties. So what if I like something a bit different? Tom Jones, Brenda Lee, Elvis and Roy Orbison. Sounds sad doesn't it but I'm happy. I couldn't give a toss what the others think.

We're going somewhere different today – Cheltenham. A few of the lads have played there before but it's new to most of us who only know it for the racing.

The trip takes a while but not as bad as the one to Swansea a few weeks before. It took us nine hours to get to the hotel after we got stuck behind four accidents. We didn't get our evening meal til 10.30.

This time the traffic's moving and we've done it before six o'clock. That's enough of Pretty Woman for now, Roy. We're eating at 6.30 like usual which is always a problem for me. I don't mind the food but it means that I won't get to see Emmerdale and Coronation Street. I love my soaps and just hope the missus has remembered to record them.

It's not much fun being stuck in a hotel the night before a game so I tend to go to bed early. I'll often be tucked up by 9pm watching TV because there's nothing else to do.

At least I've got Richard Edghill, one of the older lads, sharing the room this time. He's sound and he's tidy – which is the main thing.

I usually room with Ben Muirhead but he's injured. He's a scruffy twat who always leaves everything all over the floor. I hate that and end up following him to pick it all up. On the very rare occasions when he decides to have a shave he won't even clean the sink afterwards. So I do that as well.

I've got this obsession with the room being clean and spotless and everything put in exactly the right place. When we've got a home game, I'll always give the house a quick tidy-up before I leave for the ground.

I had to laugh at Wayne Rooney saying that he needed the sound of the hoover to help him go to sleep. I'm probably the same. I get a bit pissed off at away games because I can't do any hoovering first. Perhaps that's why I had a time when I couldn't score away from home. Blame it on having no hoover.

Everyone has their own ritual on the morning of the game. In the hotel, I'll be up about eight o'clock and nip downstairs for a cup of tea and a couple of slices of toast. Then it's back to bed in time for the start of Soccer AM which I love. I've been on the programme often enough and it makes me laugh. I'll get to see all of it before we all meet up in the dining room again for the pre-match meal. Different lads will choose different things but I stick with chicken and beans every time. Nothing too heavy and it gives me plenty of energy.

We always aim to be at the ground for 1.30, an hour and a half before kick-off. You have a little wander outside to look at the pitch and then back to the dressing room to flick through the programme and sort out any tickets for mates or your family.

Often the gaffer will give me a couple of bets to put on the horses. He thinks he's good at it but his tips cost me a fortune. Can't argue with him though, because he's in charge.

It's now coming up to 2.30 and the lads all head out for a warm-up. I'm the last one to go as usual. The others reckon I only come out late so that I'll get my own cheer from the crowd. They've started taking the piss by stopping to clap when I appear.

But it's just something I've always done through my career. A bit of a superstition if you like but unless I'm captain when I'll lead the lads out, I like to be the last one leaving the dressing room.

Before I do run out, I'll wash my face three times first. And I'll do it again before we go back out for the kick-off. I don't know why but it's just part of my pre-match ritual.

The gaffer gives his team talk and tells us how to get at the opposition and where their weaknesses are. We all chip in and wind each other up as the nerves begin to kick in.

Then the signal comes through. Five minutes to go and this is it. Let's go to work.

Cheltenham's ground isn't the best but the pitch is smart. It's early season, the sun is out, and it's a great day to play football.

We start off knocking the ball about quite well but they score with their first shot. Shit, that wasn't supposed to happen. It's becoming one of those days. We're having all the possession and creating a lot of chances but nothing is going in.

I get in a tangle with their skipper John Finnigan who ends up spinning me round on the floor. The ref has a look but doesn't do anything. Then it kicks off. He's at it again and I grab him. In the groin.

Maybe I was just feeling sexually frustrated and decided to feel his bollocks! He obviously doesn't like it and swings an elbow at me. I'm holding my face and the shit's about to hit the fan. It was away from the ball and the game is still going on but the fourth official has seen it.

He was only a few yards away from the incident and when the ball goes out, the ref is straight over. The crowd are getting wound up because they know their player is on his way. Over comes the ref and he books me. It's my first yellow card of the season. But it's a straight red for their lad and he's not happy.

The home fans are really angry about it and slag me off for the rest of the game. But that doesn't bother me because I'm used to it. To be honest, I love it, absolutely love it when I'm getting abuse off the opposition crowd. It just makes me try harder and play better and it also keeps them off the backs of the other lads in the team.

The Cheltenham manager John Ward calls me a cheat but I've done nothing wrong. I didn't get their lad sent off, he did it himself by using an elbow. Whether he connected or not, it doesn't matter. Once you raise your arm and throw an elbow like that then it's always an automatic red card. I gave him the bait and he took it. He's got only himself to blame.

Cheltenham take off one of their strikers to bring on another player in midfield but they are hanging on now. We get the equalizer straight after half-time, then hit the bar.

With 20 minutes to go, we take the lead with a great goal from our winger Jermaine Johnson. The lad's really quick and runs away from just inside their half to score.

I don't get a goal myself but I'll claim the assist for JJ because it was my pass that sent him off to the races. I'm just glad he kept on running and scored because I didn't fancy trying to keep up with him.

But it's another good away win for us, especially after going a goal down early on. Cheltenham are moaning but I don't care. The job's been done and the rest is history.

Now to get back on that coach and home in time for a couple of celebration beers.

CAREFREE DAYS?

"DEAN HAS GOT A ONE TRACK MIND and it's not maths. I hope he will not grow to regret it"

That was the summer of 1981 and one of the kinder comments on my report card.

The teachers at Francis Askew junior school in Hull all thought the same. I was disruptive, uninterested, careless and only interested in waiting for the break-time bell to go so I could have a ball at my feet.

My form teacher accused me of "sailing very close to the wind with too many members of staff". I wound them up. I didn't mean to, it's just that sitting in class never interested me. I wasn't prepared to work hard enough and every teacher knew it.

The head sussed it out. He would always comment on my lack of effort in the classroom compared with what I did on the football field. "If Dean would only work as hard in school then he would surprise us all."

But it was all sport with me. Football mainly, although I also played cricket and hockey for the school and was a pretty mean pentathlete in athletics. I was never going to be an Einstein.

Life began for me in 1969 on April Fool's Day. Yeah, I know what you're thinking. And I've played the fool ever since. Ha bloody ha. I got the mickey taken out of me at school as you'd expect. But being born on April 1 has its good points. Later in life, nobody forgets your birthday.

Hessle Road in Hull was where it all started with mum and dad, John and Doreen, and my brother Lee who was six years older. It was nothing special but we weren't poor. My dad worked on the docks as a fisherman and earned enough to put food on the table while mum stayed at home and looked after us.

When I was two we moved to an area of the city called Gipsyville, which isn't as bad as it sounds. Dad changed jobs and joined Tetley's brewery and worked there for the next 26 years as a driver.

I used to hang around with Lee all the time even though he was much older. It must have really pissed him off having his kid brother always there – I'm sure he never wanted me around but you know what I'm like.

Dad used to play in goal for a local football team called Ross Group on a Saturday. I used to go watch him every week and help put all the flags out and nets up before the game. That was where my love affair for the game started.

I'd be there at all his matches and presentation nights and made sure I was at the front of all the team photos as an unofficial mascot. I've still got the pictures in a scrapbook with dad's team showing off all the cups and me in the first row hogging the limelight – all my team-mates since will say that nothing has changed.

There were lots of photos because they were a very good team who seemed to win everything.

Right from an early age football had taken over my life and when I was nine I joined Gipsyville Boys, a junior side that had been set up by dad's mate Dave Davison. I was centre midfield and loved to be star of the show. You used to get a box of Maltesers for being the man of the match. That was all the incentive I needed – my teeth took a hammering with the number of sweets I was given.

We played on a Sunday morning so I could still go and watch a game on the Saturday. If dad wasn't playing then we'd go and watch Hull City at Boothferry Park. They were second division then and had people like Billy Whitehurst, Richard Jobson and Garry Parker – really hard guys who didn't take any prisoners.

They were struggling at the time and would get crowds of only 3,000 or 4,000. But I loved the atmosphere, sitting in the South Stand and feeling part of it.

The Hull captain then was a player called Peter Skipper and I remember the thrill of meeting him for the first time.

I got voted the player of the year in our Sunday league out of all the divisions and Skip presented me with the trophy. It was unbelievable – and I've still got the award.

It's funny now because I still see Skip for a pint every now and then and we sometimes play together for the ex-Tigers team from players who used to be at Hull. I think he's in insurance now. He must have dished out hundreds of prizes over the years and obviously can't remember this one kid in the Sunday league. But I'm still chuffed about it because he was the first footballer who presented me with a trophy.

Francis Askew had a great school team as well. A teacher called Dougie Fairlow took us and he was football mad. Dougie was our art teacher and whenever we got to a cup final or a big game he would get all the kids in lessons to make these big rosettes in the school colours. It felt as if we were going to Wembley.

He was only meant to take us in the under-11s. The next year it should have been a different teacher. But we didn't want to lose him and at the end of the term we got up a petition to keep Dougie in charge. I suppose it was an early case of player-power. But it worked and he kept with us all the way. We won all the cups and all the finals and we'd take bus-loads of kids to come and watch us – all wearing their hand-made rosettes. Dougie must have been the Alex Ferguson of Francis Askew.

Nowadays there aren't enough teachers around like him. Most aren't bothered about sport and putting in those extra hours for the kids which is a pity. The kids don't realise what they are missing out on.

As I got older, I moved on to Riley High School which was all-boys. All my mates went there and frankly I wasn't bothered about having no girls around the place. I was too young then. I had a few girlfriends from around the estate but not that many. I was more into the sport.

The football team at Riley wasn't bad but it was really a rugby school. We used to play rugby league. I played a little bit but as one of the smaller lads I kept out the way of all the rough stuff – a bit different to now.

As I said, I wasn't so keen on what went on inside the classroom. I wasn't thick but I just couldn't do the exams. It was in one ear and out the other. My work generally was okay and you never heard any real complaints at parents' evening or owt like that. It was just when it came to exams that I'd really struggle.

That was the story right through the school and in the end I just didn't take any exams. I didn't see the point and I was twagging lessons anyway.

My real problems started when I was 13 and mum and dad got divorced. It left me devastated at the time and took a long, long time to recover from. It's only now that certain people will discover how long.

You know as a kid when your mum and dad are going through a bad time. You hear things and notice what's happening though you want to block it out. But the dreaded moment came one Sunday morning when I was laying in bed next to my dad. He told me that he was leaving because he didn't love my mam any more. I burst into tears as he said that he still loved me and Lee but couldn't pretend things were all right because they weren't.

Of course, I had seen it coming but you try to block things out. My dad used to have a red Ford Capri, a newish car so it stood out a bit, and my mates at school said they'd seen him picking this dark-haired girl up in a petrol station near the playing fields.

I would never believe them until it all came out and he was having an affair with a woman who worked there. It hit me hard because I knew that he was not coming back. He moved in to my nana's house to live with his mum and I'd only see him at weekends. Margaret, the woman he left my mum for, is now his wife though he tried to keep her out of my way for a few years until things settled down.

My brother was 18 by then so he was out doing his own thing. He was working and had his own girlfriend so he'd be out with her or drinking in the pub most nights.

It was me who was left to carry the can, watching my mother crying every day. She loved my dad that much and just couldn't handle it without him.

My mum worked nights for Bird's Eye so I was left to fend for myself at home. Every night I'd lock the front door at nine and go to bed and mum would be back to wake me up for school in the morning.

It was very, very hard and things got so bad that one day she tried to kill herself by overdosing on tablets. It was terrifying seeing my mum in a state like that and I panicked and rang my dad to come round and help. She kept repeating how much she loved him and couldn't go on without him. But my dad just pushed her on the couch and said that their marriage was already over and she had to sort herself out because of me.

At the end of the day, nobody was looking after me. Dad was doing his own thing, while I was in my first year at senior school and having to watch out for mum.

Lee was flitting from pillar to post with his girlfriend, staying at her house as often as he was at home, so I was left to cope on my own at home.

There was a couple who lived over the back, Billy and Linda Christmas, who would look out for me from time to time. We didn't have any holidays but they would take me out for days and helped to make things a little easier while my mum couldn't cope.

It went on for three years and basically I had to fend for myself all that time. It was no wonder that school went out the window – I didn't go at all in the last year. My dad didn't say much but how could he? He didn't have the right to get involved because of what had gone on.

That's when I started drinking in my local pub. I was 15 or 16 at the time and pretty small for my age but the other lads used to smuggle me in the corner. The group of friends I'd knock about with were a bit older than me, the same age as my brother, and they'd sneak me into a table where nobody could see. Lads like Gary Harrison, Gary Duncan, Paul Baines and David Schultz looked after me and would get me a pint of bitter.

The landlord was called Tony Bannam, an ex-rugby player for Doncaster, and he knew that I was in there. He'd chuck me out every now and then but other times would turn a blind eye and let me stay because I was in the corner and out the way.

I'd also go into a pub called the Fiveways where I took false ID in. They went for it and thought I was 18. It was a release from all the shit going on at home and I started drinking heavily. It wasn't long before it became a problem.

My mum got a boyfriend in the end, a fella called Mick, and we never saw eye to eye. He'd come in and start shouting at me to get my feet off the chairs and things like that. But I wouldn't have it – it was my f****** house not his so what right did he have to try and throw his weight around? We would argue about anything and everything and mum made it worse by always taking his side.

To be fair, he was good to my mum and looked after her. I was grateful for that because she needed someone in her life - but I just couldn't accept that he was sleeping in my dad's bed. I never came to terms with it. My only answer was to drink. And when I had one pint, I didn't want to stop. It got to the stage where every time I got drunk, I'd peed the bed when I woke up. I was getting aggressive for no reason.

I was at home for the two years I was an apprentice at Hull and we just fought and argued the whole time. And mum would always back Mick all the way which I couldn't handle.

Things got no better when I worked on the building site with Mick still trying to tell me what to do. And it reached the point where we ended up scuffling and throwing punches because I couldn't take any more. That was the final straw for my mum. I'd just turned pro and came home one night to find my bags were all packed up and left in the porch.

I'd dared to have a go at her precious Mick and she didn't want me around anymore. It was a horrible feeling that she felt more about him than me. All the things I'd done for her when she was at her lowest point after dad had left and they'd all been thrown back in my face. But she couldn't see it and just wanted me out of her face.

What hurt just as much was Lee's reaction. My brother thought I was bang out of order for the way I was treating my mum. It took me a long time to forget that.

DEVIL'S SAUCE

SO HERE I WAS kicked out of my own home, nobody in the family wanted to know me and I had nowhere to live. I needed help from someone and turned up at Gary Duncan's door asking if I could sleep at his house for the night. I must have looked in a terrible state stood there with a couple of bags of clothes filled with my stuff and trying to explain that I'd been chucked out. Thankfully he put me up until I got my head round what was happening but eventually I went to my brother's.

Our Lee had just got married to Adele and he let me move in to their spare room, paying £20 a week in rent. It was all right until one week when I didn't pay and he just told me to f****** get out the house. Once again I had nowhere to go. My dad was living at my nana's, mum was obviously still with that bloke that I couldn't stand and there was no way I could go back there. I hated Mick's guts. He was a patronizing prick; he didn't want to know me and I didn't want him in my life – or my dad's bed.

Then one Saturday night I was out in Pepper's, a local night club in town. It was heaving in there but I bumped into Dave Davison, my first football manager for Gipsyville Boys, and his wife Pauline who were having a drink. I was a young pro at the time with Hull and they still lived right next to Boothferry Park. We got talking and I asked him what he was up to. It turned out they were doing digs for apprentices at the club and had two young lads living with them who they looked after. I saw my chance and put my cards on the table, explaining that I had nowhere to live. I was begging to move in with them. Dave said yes straight away and I was made up. I paid £50 a week but Pauline was doing all my washing and ironing and cooked the meals.

It was like being at home again. No, it was better than being at home because I didn't have all the shit going on around me. Dave and Pauline were absolutely fantastic, giving me my own key and letting me come and go as I pleased.

I met Helen, who later became my wife, and they let her stay over as well. They didn't mind her sleeping there at all. It was such a change to be living in a happy environment again where everybody got on. And it helped me get over those horrible years from 13 to about 19 or 20 when I was basically left to look after myself with nobody to turn to.

It got so bad during that time I even went round to my mates for Christmas dinner. I'm not joking but I never got invited to my mum's house or to dad's, it was horrible.

Luckily Mike Trotter, who's probably one of the best mates I've ever had, let me go there and his mum and dad made me dinner. I would sit there thinking, if only they were my parents.

All these years on, you never forget something like that. You try to shut it out and the football was a release because I was living my dream after signing pro. But the shadow of what had gone on during my teenage years was always there. And it would rear its head every time I went out for a drink.

I tried not to go out so often but every time I did it would become a massive problem.

It had become a habit to drink heavily to try and blot out my troubles at home. And once I'd had a few pints, I just couldn't seem to stop until I reached the point of no return. Then when I came home,

I'd turn the lights off and crash out in the dark, listening to Elvis music and songs that reminded me of my mum and dad.

I didn't really know what I was doing because of the beer and I'd wake up to find I had peed in the bed. But this wasn't just a one-off, it happened every time – and kept happening until I was nearly 30-years-old.

People outside didn't have a clue what was going on. But even when I was playing for Aberdeen, I'd come in from a drinking session and start smashing the house up.

I was uncontrollable when I got to that point. I was punching walls, smashing doors and taking it out on my wife.

I never hit Helen or anything like that but I know I really scared her with my behaviour. And what made it even worse is that when I woke up the next day, I wouldn't be able to remember a thing let alone why I'd done it.

I thought I must have an alcoholic problem. What I didn't know was that all this blind rage and anger inside me was caused by the feelings bottled up from all those years ago.

Once I had a skinful of beer that feeling of rejection and being abandoned would all come out. It was the switch to let off all that frustration I had tried to keep inside for so long.

Every time I had a drink, I cried, lost my temper and did bad things. And the worst thing was I couldn't understand why.

It must have been terrible for Helen. She didn't know what I was going to do next.

She used to dread me going out with the lads for a drink because she was terrified about what I was going to be like when I got home. I'd wake up in the morning and see holes in the wall but I couldn't believe that it was me doing that. If people came round the house, I'd put up the paintings that Josh had done at nursery just to cover up the damage so that nobody would notice.

I was in a state of denial but something had to be done. Our lives couldn't go on like this with me acting this way. I was ruining everything and hated myself for the way I was behaving. Luckily help was round the corner thanks to Stuart Hogg. He was our full-time fitness coach at Aberdeen but also used to teach athletics and trained my wife every day.

She was a sprinter and used to run in the Scottish AAA championships so Stuart would work with her all the time.

Obviously he could see that she wasn't happy and when he asked, Helen told him everything. Stuart put me in touch with Richard Cox, a psychologist in Edinburgh and I went to see him for six or seven sessions.

It was hard at first because nobody wants to go and see a shrink. I was embarrassed.

All these thoughts were going round my head. Why did I need therapy? Am I depressed? Am I a bad person? Or am I going totally mad? The last place on earth I wanted to go was to see this bloke. But I had to find out what was triggering all these problems. I wanted to ask him why I was so aggressive and why I was peeing the bed.

I said straight away that I had a drink problem but he wasn't so sure. He wanted me to tell him the whole story. That's when it all came out. It was the first time that I'd ever really spoken so openly and it felt such a relief just to let it all gush out. I just couldn't stop crying as I talked. But I wasn't embarrassed. Richard was great, reassuring me that it was a natural reaction and told me to keep going. He was clear that I didn't have a drink problem. It was just that when I drank too much it brought all my bad memories flooding back and that would drive the anger.

Seeing Richard was a breath of fresh air. Suddenly all my troubles were clear to me, it was like someone had opened this window and I could see again. He didn't tell me to stop drinking, I don't think I could have handled that. But he did suggest that after I've had two or three bottles of beer to stop and have a glass of water. That would calm it down a bit and it helped me.

My family life was getting better and I owe that to Stuart. If it wasn't for him sorting me out with Richard then I dread to think where I might have ended up because it was getting seriously bad. What was making me more angry was that nobody else in the family thought there was anything wrong. Mum, dad and our Lee didn't know anything about the shrink, the alcohol, the anger problem – all they could see was that Dean was playing professional football and earning big money and everything was rosy in the garden.

Nobody asked and I didn't want to tell them. I never even spoke to my mum for three years because of Mick and it was only after he died that she wanted to come back in my life again. Our relationship is good now but it took time. She couldn't just expect everything to be fine straight away after all that had gone on. Helen had seen everything and she was more bitter towards my mum than anybody because she knew what it had done to me.

BOOTHFERRY BARRACKS

I LIKE TO THINK I HAVEN'T CHANGED over the years. People might see the big-shot footballer with loads of money and a big car but I'm still the same Dean Windass around my mates.

It's just the way life pans out and you go your separate ways, especially when you're in football.

My life started to change the day I walked into Boothferry Park as an apprentice. It felt like I was joining the army for two years. Despite what was happening at home, I was a confident 16-year-old ready to take on the world but that didn't stop the nerves on the first morning. There were 14 of us, strangers from other towns, all wondering what was about to happen. The only familiar face was Mike Smith, who used to play in the Hull boys team with me. He's my brother-in-law now.

I had been getting picked for Hull school teams since I was ten. From the time I got picked for the Hull Boys under-11s, I was always dreaming about slipping on that Tigers jersey. We used to wear an amber shirt that was quite similar so even in those early days in my mind I could imagine me stepping out at Boothferry Park and the roar of the crowd.

I got called to the front of school assembly at Francis Askew the first time I got picked for Hull Boys. The whole room cheered as I shook hands with the headmaster – and at that moment I knew all I wanted to do when I grew up was to be a footballer. I loved the adulation. Some will say nothing has changed since.

There were kids from all different schools in the representative side but it wasn't a problem because most of the same faces were there every year as we got older. But at the age of 12, the coaches decided that I was better than most of the other lads in the under-14s so I was put in the team the year ahead.

That was a really big thing at the time, especially as I was the smallest kid in the side. Luckily I had the skill to survive and do well against lads who were both older and bigger than me. Not only that, they made me captain which was a massive achievement. You never forget that feeling of leading the team out before a match. It might have looked a bit funny seeing this little kid bossing all the others about. But then I've always had a big mouth so that was never a problem.

We didn't get many people coming to see us but we knew there might be a scout from a football club around. My dad always used to tell me that you never know who might be watching. We'd joke about only one man and his dog bothering to watch the game but that bloke walking his pet round the park might have been the guy from the football club. So I was always aware of who was around every time we kicked off.

People started coming up to my dad to ask about me and there were scouts from Sheffield and Leeds who were interested. But Hull also spotted me and after that it was no contest. They didn't have academies as such back then but I signed on schoolboy forms which meant that I wasn't allowed to go anywhere else. Not that I'd have done that anyway.

Why would I ever want to leave Boothferry Park? This was the only place that I wanted to be.

So here I was at Hull with all the other young wannabe football stars like me. People like Neil Buckley, who went on to play for Hull and Ian Sampson, who made it at Sunderland. Looking back now, it was run like a military regime but nobody was complaining. After all, this is what all of us had dreamed of.

We had to be in for 9am every day to begin our chores. You had to work first and then play later. And if you didn't do your job right, then you were made to start all over again.

I was the boot man and had to make sure every player had clean footwear. It's not like nowadays when two apprentices get to look after one pro; it was just me and a dressing room full of mud-splattered boots.

Some mornings it was horrendous. It wasn't just boots either, you would also get lumped with trainers and everything. To make it even worse, I'd have big Billy Whitehurst breathing down my neck to make sure the stripes on his boots were gleaming. And you didn't want to get on the wrong side of him. Any mud crusted round the studs or on the laces and the boots would be hurled back at you to do again. He was one scary bastard.

And yet it was quite a cushy number compared with what some of the other apprentices had to do. I wouldn't have swapped it. I used to lock the boot room when I was working and put the heater on in there. It was nice and toasty while some of the other poor bastards were sweeping the stands in the freezing weather.

I took real pride in my work, especially knowing that the longer I took, the less chance there was of being called outside to help with the cleaning. The lads used to hammer me because I was tucked up nice and warm every day while they had socks round their hands to try and keep the cold out. Well someone's got to do it!

Mind you, those socks came in handy when you were put on toilet duty. The thicker the better when you had to put your hand down the bowl and scrape out all the shit. And they say football is all glamour.

I used to envy all the pros when they came in from their training.

A quick shower and they were going home while we were left to clean up behind them. One day, I would say to myself, that will be me. I'll be heading home just after lunch and leaving my crap for someone else to sweep up. That was a great incentive.

You couldn't mix with the senior boys much. There were strict rules about that, just like the army again. You couldn't walk into the first-team dressing room without knocking. That was an absolute no no. You had to ask permission first – otherwise you paid a heavy penalty. Big Billy and Skip would pin you down on the side and black your bollocks with dubbin. It was no good trying to resist because they were too strong as they stripped you naked and smeared boot polish all over your privates. I'd come home with a black dick nearly every day.

It sounds cruel but that was all part of the education. The real world of professional football. It's changed dramatically now. The kids still clean the boots but there are kit men who sort out the shirts and the rest. And you don't see much dubbin about.

We had to do everything, mop the floors, clean the bath out. You name it, we did it.

But it was great for discipline. You had to muck in or they'd kick you out.

Neil Buckley was our top man. He was our elected shop steward, our leader, and at the end of each day he would go to the manager and tell him that our jobs were done.

But the coaches could be bastards. They would come out for an inspection and look for any little thing. They would run a finger along the top of the door to see if there was any dust. And if one finger was mucky, you'd be sent back to do the whole changing room again. They were taking the piss but it was a test. Looking back, you realise why they did it. If you didn't do your job right then you were letting the rest of the team down. Just like on a Saturday.

Taking a short cut with the cleaning was no different to not making the effort during a match. Did you track a runner? Are you marking properly at corners? In the same way, if you never cleaned the rim of the toilet you were letting your team-mates down. It was all part of creating that team ethic. And it worked because you never wanted to disappoint anybody.

For my second year, Andy Payton took over from Neil as our leader. He loved it and would strut around the place with a stick under his arm like a real sergeant major. I'm sure he imagined he was drilling us to go off to battle somewhere. But that time must have rubbed off on me. If you look at my home now, it's spotless.

My wife and kids will tell you that I hate untidiness and I think that stemmed from those years as an apprentice. I don't go as far as checking the door frame for dust, though. The missus would give me a belt across the face if I even thought of trying that.

It may have sounded a very strict regime at Hull but I loved it. They treated you like adults and between 16 and 18 I grew up very quickly. I was getting paid £26.50 a week for the first year and then £35 for the second. I used to put £10 in my pension, which you had to do through the Professional Footballers' Association, and I'd give my mum £5 board. The rest of the money just disappeared.

I thought I was rich when it went up the second year. But what I didn't realise was that the pension had doubled as well so I didn't have any more cash in my pocket.

But the money didn't matter. The only goal of being an apprentice is to prove to the club that you can cut it as a pro. Those two years were all about showing that you had to be kept on.

Everything was under scrutiny, whether you were training and playing matches or doing a decent job shining someone's size eights. The club were watching you just as closely off the field as on it. It was about a lot more than having the ability to do things on the pitch. You had to show the same attitude clearing the stands or cleaning boots.

Of course, by the second year I started getting twitchy. Everyone did because this was the big one. Who was going to be taken on and which poor bastards would be shown the door?

FROZEN DREAMS

I HAD A BIG PROBLEM. Or rather, in my case, it was a small one. At that age size does matter and I was one of the tiniest in the group. So much so that at 17 I still didn't have any pubes on my bollocks. I was a very late developer and the lads would take the piss out of me.

I used to get in the bath and hide in the corner, making sure I kept well away from the ones who were much better endowed. I'd sit there crouched up with my hands over my privates and wait until everyone else had gone. Then I'd jump out and shove a towel round me as quickly as possible. It was embarrassing and the lads had a laugh. But the stick I got was in fun and was all part of growing up.

My small frame was a worry though. I had the ability to make the grade but physically I wasn't strong enough. And when the big day came, that was what counted against me.

It was the morning that we had all been dreading. Brian Horton, the manager, called the lads into his office one by one and told them whether they would be offered a contract or not. Sitting outside was worse than being in the dentist's waiting room. Everyone sat there with their own thoughts, waiting for the moment when their name would be called.

The first five or six weren't taken on. Then things started looking up. Andy Payton came back out with his thumbs up, he was all right.

Leigh Jenkinson was the same and Mike Smith, Les Thompson, Gavin Kelly, Neil Buckley. They were all given a year's contract.

You didn't know how many players the manager planned to take on. But I hoped that after rejecting the first lot, this was a good sign. I was the last one to be called. I sat down opposite Brian Horton and he asked me how I felt I had done. I had started scoring a few goals recently in the youth team after being pushed up front so things were going well. Or so I thought. He listened and then dropped the bombshell. "I'm sorry, but we're not keeping you on."

They were looking for people capable of pushing for the first team the following season and I didn't look strong enough. Everything in my game was there but I didn't have the physical side needed. Dennis Booth, the assistant manager, had made the decision. He reckoned I had plenty of talent and enthusiasm but no legs. I'd be great if you were playing football in the living room but no good on a full-size pitch.

I could feel myself welling up as the gaffer spoke. Then the tears flowed. It's a moment I will never forget until the day I die.

Being a footballer is all I'd ever wanted to be. That dream had been destroyed by someone telling me that I wasn't good enough. As I wiped my eyes and shook his hand, he said something else. Something that has always stuck with me. Brian Horton said: "I know that you'll prove me wrong."

Looking back now, I wasn't ready to make the grade. He was right. I didn't have the strength to cope with playing against men every week. I'd have been brushed off the ball too easily. I was a lightweight and wouldn't have got away with it. The other lads who got taken on weren't better players than me but they were more mature physically. They were strong enough to get box to box if the gaffer suddenly threw them in the first team the next year. There was no way in the world that I would have been able to do that.

If he had given me that year's contract it would not have helped him or me. Putting it simply, I'd have been released a year later. But at that time, it felt like my world had ended. I didn't want to go back to real life.

They say that football is the land of milk and honey but my road to success was covered in rice and peas. Forget the glitz and glamour, there is nothing Premiership about packing frozen food for Bird's Eye. Not that I saw my first day in the packet rice industry as a step towards a career as a successful player. As far as I was concerned, the game had already broken my heart.

My mates still had their dreams through football. Me? I was packing rice and peas.

With the hurt still burning from Hull's rejection, I had to get myself a job. I needed to earn a few bob somewhere.

My mum worked at Bird's Eye and put in a good word for me. She pulled a few strings and I got a seasonal job which was usually reserved just for students.

I spent every day for six months packing peas, taking them out of a big truck, weighing them off and then sticking them through a processing machine. Talk about job satisfaction. Thankfully it couldn't last forever and when the pea season finished, so did my involvement. Then I graduated on to rice.

Dad's best friend sorted me out for a shift in the industrial estate near our home. This time I was putting rice down a giant hopper for the women at the bottom to pack into containers. Somehow I managed to stick that out for a year. But all the time I struggled to keep my footballing dream alive. There had to be much more to life than shoving frozen veg into a big, black hole.

I felt I could have been heading the same way. But I refused to give up on football.

I'm sure, deep down, Brian Horton knew I could do it and so did my dad. "It's only one man's opinion," had been his level-headed reaction to my world-shattering news from Hull City. "There are plenty more fish in the sea." And some were over the sea.

Dad knew a bloke who played for a French team in Montpelliers. They were called Ales although it was a better standard than the pub league which I played in every Sunday morning. They invited me over for two weeks to see what I thought. But I was very young, only 18, and barely lasted five days before I was pleading to come home.

I shared a dormitory with three local lads but I couldn't speak French and they didn't know English. It was a right barrel of laughs. I felt lost and lonely and home-sick for Hull. Yes, it was football but this was not how I wanted it.

When I returned to England, Dad put my name about a bit and I was invited for a trial with York City by their manager Bobby Saxton. I was still working on the rice at the time but the boss was good about it and gave me time off so I could go training.

York went well and for seven months I trained regularly with the club and even played a few times in the reserves. Then Bobby pulled me off the training pitch one day. I recognised the expression straight away. It was the same face Brian Horton had pulled. Only this time, it was nothing to do with my build. Unfortunately York were in a big hole financially and they had to get rid of players rather than bring any in.

The same thing happened after a week with Cambridge United. That looked a good club with Chris Turner in charge and Dion Dublin playing in the reserves but again money was too tight. I had a reserve game against Orient and then it was back home to Hull again with head down.

I like to think now that weaker people would have jacked it in at that point. But giving up has never been in my nature. There were 92 clubs in the Football League after all. Surely one of them would give me a break. I put letters out to all of them, pleading my case. I got one reply from Scarborough saying they weren't taking on any trialists.

The rice was pissing me off just like the peas had done. I couldn't even look at a curry. Then a mate I would go drinking with said he could get me a job on the building sites. Nothing fancy but plenty of fresh air and exercise – and no bloody frozen veg to worry about.

They were working on a new house. Having knocked down the old one, it was my responsibility to clean the bricks and wipe all the rubbish and shit off so they could be recycled. As I say, it was no grand job but it was a step up from shovelling rice. And the money was better too. My basic pay in the factory was £101 a week and I'd take home £81 of that. On the building site that rose to £180 of which £140 was mine. Things were slowly looking up.

On the football front, I'd signed for North Ferriby who were a decent non-league team just outside Hull. They paid me £50 a game with an extra £15 as a win bonus. I was getting some money in my pocket. But another trial came and went. This time at Sunderland under Denis Smith.

He took me up there for a fortnight and I played two reserve games. Then came the same, old lines from the manager about cutting costs, tightening belts. The usual crap way of saying thanks, but no thanks. I was 20, an age when most lads in the game had signed their first professional contracts. But there was me with my nose pressed against the window, stuck on the outside and desperate to get in.

It would have been easier to go out drinking with my mates and get pissed after work like they did. But that little voice of hope in the back of my mind kept driving me on. If I was going to make it though, I had to become fitter and stronger.

I would work from 7am to 4.30pm on the site, hod-carrying and mixing gear for brickies. It was knackering but that didn't stop me going out training as soon as I got home. I'd be straight back out on mum's porch in my running shorts. Just remembering the embarrassment of not being able to keep up with the other apprentices at Hull kept me going. There was no way I would ever go through that again.

So whatever the weather, I'd be out there pounding the streets and giving it everything. Often I'd be that tired, I'd come home, have a bath and be in bed by 6.30 which wasn't much fun for the girl I was seeing at the time. Doing that for five days and then playing football on Saturday and Sunday was my week. But it had to be done.

My big break came on the Friday after I'd been to see Denis Smith. Dad picked up the phone and it was Nicky Barmby's old man Geoff. He worked at Boothferry Park as an electrician and knew the manager Terry Dolan who had been asking about me. Hull's chief scout Bernard Ellison had seen me playing for Ferriby and put in a good word with Terry. They offered me a month to prove myself.

I had to square it with the site boss Chris Cooper first to have the time off and he was great about it. After all, this wasn't just any club – this was Hull. The following day I played for North Ferriby and then on the Monday morning I went down to the ground to meet Terry.

I didn't know it at the time but Terry had made up his mind about me within 20 minutes of the first training session. I was mixing it with the senior boys and he'd seen enough there and then to offer me a three-year contract.

He put me in the team for the reserve game at home to Grimsby the next night and it felt like being picked for the cup final. Suddenly everything had changed. One minute I was being shown the door by Sunderland, the next Geoff Barmby was on the phone to say that Hull wanted me.

We beat Grimsby 2-1 and I thought the game had gone well. All the pros were off the following day but Terry wanted to see me. I had a pint with Dad in the local Gipsyville Tavern that night not knowing what to expect. I'd been that used to setbacks and disappointments but it was impossible not to build my hopes up.

And the following morning my dream came true. With a big smile, Terry put the contract on the table. I would get £250 a week for the first year, rising to £300 for the second and £325 the third. But it wasn't about money. I would have signed on that dotted line for £50. I just wanted to play football so badly. No more slaving away on a building site, no more bricks, peas, rice. Hull City here I come.

You learn to appreciate life in football when you've seen it from the outside. Many players don't know they're born because everything is done for them and they don't have to think for themselves. But coming into the game late, I knew all about hard work. I'd slogged my guts out for £100 a week, been the general dogsbody for every brickie and then pounded the streets every evening. Now I was just training two hours a day, it was a Godsend.

Some never get a second chance but I grabbed mine. I'll always be grateful to Terry Dolan for being the one who said yes. He knew I had it in me and had the faith to let me prove it. And there was the incentive to prove Brian Horton wrong. Dad was right, it was only one man's view and who can say you're not good enough if you believe that you are?

THE PRO

IT WAS REAL Madrid, Manchester United, Liverpool and Arsenal all rolled into one. At last I was playing for Hull, my team.

I made my debut in the League Cup, or Rumbelows as it was called at the time. QPR away and we were up against it because they were First Division. I was playing in midfield and had to pinch myself when I saw the names I would be facing.

They had a great midfield four, Ray Wilkins, Ian Holloway, Andy Sinton wide on the left and Andy Impey on the right. Not to mention Les Ferdinand and Gary Thompson up front. It was no surprise we got the run-around and were hammered 5-1. But despite the scoreline it just felt brilliant to be playing. Dean Windass was officially a professional footballer.

Technically, I was still a trialist because I had not had the chance to sign on the dotted line at that point. That magic moment came on Thursday, October 24, 1991, the morning after I had scored on my home debut against Bradford in the Autoglass Trophy. I got the equaliser with a good finish from the edge of the box and Mick Matthews, another Ferriby old boy, got the winner. I was in seventh heaven. Everybody was there, all my family and friends and it was a wonderful feeling to have scored at Boothferry Park.

There wasn't many there, probably only about 3,000, but it felt like 30,000 for me. I didn't have any goal celebration worked out. I just remember going mad. I'd always dreamed of playing and scoring for Hull and here I was, achieving both under the floodlights. Unbelievable!

As well as Mick, I knew some of the players in the dressing room from my time there as an apprentice. Some of the lads taken on when I got released were now in the first team so it felt a bit weird to be seeing them again. They must have thought they'd seen the back of me but here I was again. Not too many players get invited back to a club that had shown them the door.

You also had the senior boys like Russ Wilcox, who was captain, David Norton, Leigh Palin and Ken DeMange and a few of them couldn't get in the team because I was playing.

Terry knew I was determined to make the most of every day. He had experienced the same thing at 17 when Bradford bombed him – he ended up going back there as a player and the manager. There are two ways you can respond to news like that. Give up and moan about it or get your head down and fight back. I wasn't going to let this second chance slip through my fingers. Terry says to this day that I'm the player with the most natural ability that he has ever dealt with. And he knew that whatever position I'd be playing, I would not let him down.

At the time I was playing centre midfield with a lad called Gareth Stoker. We had a good season, finishing just above mid-table, and I was getting some good press. I even did one of those player profiles in the local paper where you list your favourite film, meal and whatever. One of the questions was what would you be if you weren't a professional footballer. A clown in the circus, I answered. Some will probably say that I am. But the honest answer is that I didn't know anything else. If it wasn't football, then forget it. I'd had my taste of the real world, shifting bricks and packing frozen peas and there was no way I was ever going back.

Apparently word was getting round about this useful lad at Hull and a few scouts started to appear in the stand. Even Howard Wilkinson, whose Leeds team were top of the league, had been spotted but Terry said they were all wasting their time.

Life was just as good off the pitch as I got married to Helen, who was a well-known local athlete. Her brother Darren France was at Hull and we'd been going out for just over a year. She said it wasn't love at first sight but I must have grown on her. Her dad reckoned she tamed me.

We were away on holiday in Greece when I read about Nicky Barmby getting married in a register office in Beverley. We were going to have a big do the next year but Helen was pregnant with Josh so we decided to follow suit.

As well as a married man, I also became a striker when we were hit by injuries.

Steve Moran, the former Southampton player, had a calf problem and was out for ages. He ended up having an operation. Then Chris Hargreaves toppled over in training and chipped a bone in his leg. So we had no fit strikers and were due to play Plymouth in midweek.

I always used to play up front in five-a-sides in training so Terry decided I was the obvious replacement. It was no problem for me, I'd have played anywhere.

We won the game 2-0 and I scored both. That was it, I was now the main man.

I was playing up front alongside Linton Brown and we hit it off straight away. He was a quicker, more instinctive player while I was better at holding the ball up and bringing others into play. It worked a treat.

The next game we won 4-3 at Cambridge and I scored three of them – the first hat-trick by a Hull player for four years. It was a great day and I even remember joining in with our fans in a chorus of "Knees up, Linton Brown" before a corner was being taken.

Cambridge pissed me off afterwards by trying to take the match ball off me but they weren't having it. And a week later, my collection had doubled when I got another hat-trick against Bristol Rovers. Their number two was Dennis Booth, the bloke who had let me go as an apprentice at Hull, but he was the first to come up and shake my hand afterwards.

It was an incredible time for everyone. We'd only played five games but Hull were top of the table with 13 points and I was leading scorer in the country with nine goals.

Soon after, I picked up another first. My first red card.

We were playing Bradford in a Yorkshire derby and it started brilliantly with me scoring after 30 seconds. But my game only lasted 11 minutes as I had a go at Jeff Winter and he sent me off for foul and abusive language. At least we went on to win the game 3-1. But it was not to be the last time that Bradford fans saw me heading for an early bath.

It was all happening that season. We played an FA Cup game at non-league Runcorn which had to be abandoned after the wall collapsed because of our fans celebrating a goal. I got my third hat-trick against Barnet and then celebrated Josh's birth by scoring the winner at Fulham.

The transfer rumours were growing and I was interested to find out what was going on. Like any footballer, you want to be kept informed and I'd be on the phone to Terry every day to hear if anything was happening. There were five or six clubs who kept cropping up and it was no secret that Hull needed the money. Terry didn't want to lose me but he wasn't stupid. He was just hoping to hang on to me as long as possible.

We had a great relationship – we still do to this day. He knew I was a bit of a joker but just let me get on with it. Once we were going down south to play Bristol Rovers and Bournemouth. We were playing Rovers at Bath on the Wednesday and then in Bournemouth on the Saturday so the club decided it was cheaper for us to stay down for both rather than keep going up and down the motorway. Anyway, the weather was shit. It was snowing heavily on the day of the Bristol Rovers game and the referee called it off mid-afternoon.

Everybody was feeling pretty pissed off because there was nowt to do so Terry decided we should drive down to Bournemouth a day early. He wouldn't let us have any cans on the coach but said we could have a beer or two when we got to the hotel in Christchurch.

We met down at the bar just after nine and were told we could have a few pints. Terry also suggested we relieved the boredom by playing a few silly team games. They were daft things but everyone was getting into it and, as usual, I started getting cheeky. Terry put up with it for a while but then decided I'd done enough and made me move my seat into the corner of the room and stay there like a naughty schoolboy.

Once you've learned how to behave properly, he said, then you can come back and join in again!

I knew he wasn't being serious but I did as I was told though I couldn't stay quiet for long. I had a few wisecracks back until Terry stopped the game again and told me that they would not continue until I faced the wall! The other lads were pissing themselves as I sat there facing the wall like a kid in detention. But every now and again I'd glance round and pull a stupid face to get them laughing and eventually Terry couldn't keep a straight face any longer and let me return.

He knew what I meant to the team as a player and, though he would never say it, I must have been the first name on his sheet every week. But we all knew the pressure on him to sell was growing and it got to the stage where I was left out of one game away to Brighton and I had to pretend I wasn't well. Terry was just trying to put the other clubs off the scent.

Southampton were rumoured to have offered £250,000 for me although they denied it when asked by the press. "I wouldn't know

Dean Windass if he walked into my office now," said Lawrie McMenemy, who was their director of football with Alan Ball at the time.

But Hull were holding out for big money. If they did have to lose me then they wanted more than double what Southampton were talking about.

I was still a Hull player at the end of the season and finished with 24 goals. But it was frustrating that we missed out on promotion having started so well. We didn't even make the play-offs which was down to the financial situation at the club.

Terry brought in big Ian Ormondroyd from Leicester, Ray Wallace from Reading and Burnley's Warren Joyce on loan to give us that boost and you could see the difference. We were doing really well but sadly couldn't afford to keep any of them. So by the time we got to the final game, all three of those players were back with their clubs. I still talk to Terry now about it. If those three had still been playing for us there's no way we would have missed out.

Stix Ormondroyd was a great lad. He was a big hitter from the Premier League but he won't forget his time at Boothferry Park. On his first day of training, we were practising in a circle and he cracked his head. It needed five stitches which was a good start. Anyway, we were in the showers afterwards and Stix was washing his hair with his eyes shut. I knew him a bit from playing against him in his Bradford days and thought I'd bring him back down to earth. So I pissed down his leg. He took it in good heart to be fair, and still laughs about it, but it was just my way of welcoming him to Hull!

We were a good pairing up front, little and large, but obviously he was earning big money at the time and we couldn't afford to keep him on. It was a shame because he was a big lad, always a threat to defenders with his height and I scored a hell of a lot of goals through Stix.

I was probably the biggest character in the dressing room but there were others. Gareth Stoker was supposed to be the next David Batty. But he was a bit of a weirdo.

He was the tidiest man in the world. He'd come in the changing rooms and fold his socks up, he'd put his laces in a straight line next to his shoes, he was obsessed. We'd all stagger in after training in our sweaty gear and Gareth would still fold up his dirty clothes before laying them down neatly in the skip to be washed. Gareth had been released by Leeds and Terry had picked him up. He was a great little competitor and used to buzz around the pitch like a bee in a bottle. He would chase anything and everything, a Robbie Savage type.

But we had a good blend of youth and experience. Russ Wilcox and David Norton were steady at the back and we had the players to match anyone.

I remember beating Huddersfield 1-0 at home with a Richard Peacock goal. There were 13,000 in the ground and the atmosphere was superb. When Richard scored, I ran across to the dug-out and jumped on Terry. Unfortunately I knocked the glasses off his head and he spent the next five minutes scrabbling around trying to find them. But that was a massive win for us. Huddersfield were right up there as well with Andy Booth banging in the goals so to beat them had us all convinced we would make it.

Unfortunately it turned into a nearly year because we couldn't keep those three players.

But the money problems were growing. And being the leading scorer and main asset at the time, Terry had to sell me.

Hull owed the Inland Revenue £250,000 and needed the cash fast. The story was that I was supposed to be going to Norwich where Martin O'Neill was very keen on me. I was valued at £600,000 but their chairman Robert Chase wanted to pay the fee in instalments and appearances. Hull needed at least £250,000 of that up front to pay off the tax man so the deal never happened. I understand it was the last straw for O'Neill who resigned from Norwich soon afterwards because he wasn't allowed to sign me.

Funnily enough, they got Ashley Ward instead from Crewe and we ended up playing up front together for Bradford in the Premier League.

But Norwich pulling out left me in an awkward situation because our chairman Martin Fish had told me to put my house up for sale. I sold it straight away to a squaddie but then the transfer move fell through. It was coming up to Christmas and everyone was in limbo. But Terry was very good and told me to hang on in there. He was confident something would come up quickly.

We got knocked out of the FA Cup and played shit. Terry was furious about the performance and put the whole team down for the next reserve game on the Thursday.

I was at home preparing for the game when the phone rang. It was Terry telling me I wasn't playing. I asked him why and he explained that another club had come in for me. Not only that, but they had already agreed a fee.

I was joining Aberdeen.

My mind was full of mixed emotions because I didn't really want to leave Hull and I'd only just signed a new, improved contract. But the club had to offload me, especially as they were getting the £600,000 up front.

I know Terry and the chairman got loads of stick from the supporters about it but they had no choice. Hull went through two winding-up orders before I was sold. Without that money from Aberdeen, the club would have folded. I had lived the dream with Hull. Now it was time to step up the ladder.

ENGLISH
BASTARD

"WHERE THE F**** HELL** is Aberdeen?" Those were my exact words to Terry. I knew it was in Scotland but that was about it. North, south, east, west? I didn't have a clue. Don't forget to dig out your passport, he said. I think he was taking the piss.

I still went to the reserve game that night to watch and we had an in-depth chat about the move. I spoke to the Aberdeen manager Roy Aitken and they were offering me a decent package.

So 5.30am the next morning I was getting on the plane at Humberside Airport. Terry came with me and we both met Roy at the other end. He took us to the ground for a look, we agreed personal terms and I was an Aberdeen player by the Friday afternoon. My feet had hardly touched the ground.

It didn't take much to persuade me. I was disappointed the Norwich move didn't happen but this was a big club who had played in the European Cup not that long ago. I had my first training session and the next day I was off to Glasgow for the game against Partick Thistle where I was sub.

Hull weren't playing so Terry stayed up to watch the match and take me back to Hull afterwards for an engagement party I was going to. Aberdeen even leant us the car to get there.

We had our captain Stewart McKimmie sent off before Roy threw me on. We were losing 1-0 but the reception from the away fans was magnificent. Even when I was warming up on the touchline, you could hear the shouts of "Deano, Deano" which boosted my confidence because this was a massive step for me.

I had a chance soon after coming on. Duncan Shearer flicked the ball on and I bombed through ready to make it a dream debut but put it wide. But Aberdeen were a good club and I settled into my new life quickly.

My wife Helen was brilliant about moving north. She understood the situation and with Josh, our eldest son, only two at the time we didn't have to worry about schools. It was very difficult for her at first because she didn't know anybody. All she used to do in the first couple of weeks was take Josh to the park.

But the club couldn't do enough for us and all the ironing and washing was done by the hotel.

After training, the other lads would drive me round looking for houses. Brian Mitchell, an Aberdonian who played for Hull, put me in touch with a solicitor and I managed to get fixed up within three weeks. Roy Aitken couldn't believe how quickly I had settled. But it was important for me and Helen in particular to find a place of our own.

Once we started going to the games, Helen would mingle with the other wives and it wasn't long before she loved the place. Aberdeen was a beautiful, clean city and I don't think she wanted to leave. It was bloody cold but you soon got used to it. When it snowed, it came down big style but would disappear just as fast. You could head off for training in the morning fighting through a blizzard. And yet by lunchtime it was gone because of the salt air from the sea.

The physios would take you down to the seafront if you were coming back from injury. When I had a bad ankle, they'd make me walk in the water instead of putting ice on it. The sea was colder than any ice block.

That Aberdeen team was a good one and we'd always be third in the league. You could never get any higher of course because of Celtic and Rangers although we always had tight games.

We had some real quality in the side with Billy Dodds scoring for fun alongside Duncan Shearer. Eoin Jess was a young lad coming through, Steve Glass and Paul Bernard had just signed, Stewart McKimmie captained Scotland and Jim Leighton was great in the goals.

I arrived the week after we'd won the Coca-Cola Cup against Dundee at Hampden Park so everyone was buzzing. It was a great time to be part of it. I quickly got used to the chants of "You English bastard" at every ground we played it. I don't get bothered by things like that.

They were fun times and the matches against the Old Firm clubs were extra special.

The first time I played against Rangers was at Pittodrie and the place was heaving. We were already on the pitch warming up when Rangers ran out. Paul Gascoigne would always come out last and the noise from their fans when he appeared was amazing.

But I couldn't stop looking at him. I was so in awe. I couldn't believe I was on the same pitch as Gazza. Playing for Hull one week and now up against a World Cup legend, the best midfielder in the world at that time. My wife had noticed my reaction. She said I'd spent most of the game just staring at him like some kind of stalker.

The first time he got the ball, Gazza nutmegged me. I don't think he put a foot wrong all game. But from that day on we had a good relationship. Maybe it's because we had a similar build and I looked a bit like him. People used to say I reminded them of Gascoigne because I was daft and stupid. I was probably the Gazza of Aberdeen.

That was the Rangers side that won nine titles in a row. McCoist,

Laudrup, McCall, Gascoigne, Gough, Goram … their team sheet was terrifying. The game-plan for going to Ibrox had to be perfect or you would never get a kick. You'd be beat before the kick-off. Again there would be 45,000 slating the "f****** English bastard" in the Aberdeen shirt and the noise would be deafening.

They had to win one game against us to win the league. I was playing in midfield again and told to man-mark Gazza. He was f****** outstanding and got a hat-trick. He'd scored a wonder free-kick but we were drawing 1-1. Then I saw Richard Gough looking at him as if to say "c'mon Gazza, it's up to you." He went past me as if I wasn't there and ran on and on. He went the full length of the pitch and then bent the ball into the top corner with his left foot. It was a blinding goal.

They got a penalty with five minutes to go. Coisty was their usual taker but Gazza got it to clinch his hat-trick. They'd won the league and at the end I gave Gazza a kiss. It had been a pleasure to mark him – well, if I'd managed to get the ball it would have been. I've seen him at a few dinners since and he came down to Bradford a couple of years ago for Stuart McCall's testimonial. He's someone I'll always admire. I've looked up to Gazza since he was the hero in the World Cup in Italy and maybe I have tried to model myself on him.

When I was an apprentice at Hull, Dennis Booth used to tell me to always play with a smile on my face and try to entertain people. Let's face it, football is meant to be fun and exciting to watch and nobody wants to see two teams of robots going through the motions all grumpy and that. Dennis was a character when we were kids and so was Gazza. I didn't try to copy him, it was just the way I was.

We all love playing football so why shouldn't that show? You're a long time dead so go out there and express yourself and have a laugh while you're doing it. You do something daft on the pitch and it gives the supporters a bit of a giggle. But they will remember that and it stands out from the norm.

I sometimes wonder what people will say about me when I finally hang up my boots. Something along the lines of "Deano was a daft bastard, but he could play a bit". That would do me.

I've never been the best player in the world but I've always given my all. I'm not quick but I like to think that I'm sharp upstairs. Look at players like Teddy Sheringham and Mark Hughes, both great strikers who certainly weren't the fastest. But they had the football brain and could get hold of the ball and bring other people in to play. Gazza wasn't quick. He used to be quicker running with the ball than without it because of his strength and attitude towards the game.

I always used to be told he was the fittest lad on the training ground at Rangers. Looking at him, you'd laugh but you don't all have to be built like a greyhound. I'm the same. I like to stay fit and love training. When it comes to the big runs in pre-season, I'll always be up there at the front of the pack. The enjoyment is there because you're coming in every day and having a laugh. Of course, it's a serious business but the craic in the dressing room and the piss-taking make it a special environment.

Our fitness coach at Aberdeen would tell us that the harder we trained and the more dedicated we were, the longer we would play for. That's something I try now to instil into the kids. Yeah, you can go and have a drink and nobody loves a few pints more than me. But you've got to do it at the right time. If you're training hard and then get pissed up on your day off, you've got to be prepared to work it off the following morning. And that's what I used to do. It's no good going through the motions because that's not kidding anyone.

I certainly feel fit enough to keep playing until I'm 40 or more. Stuart McCall's done it and Teddy Sheringham and I know I can carry on along the same lines. After all, you're a long time retired.

SENT PACKING

HERE'S A TRIVIA QUESTION. Name the only player to get three red cards in the same match. Yep, yours truly managed that against Dundee United. It's known as being sent off in style.

I don't know what it was about me and Dundee but it wasn't my favourite town. I got sent off seven times in three years at Aberdeen and most of them were against either Dundee or Dundee United.

Our manager Roy Aitken was under massive pressure. We were struggling and he knew that a bad result at Tannadice would probably mean the bullet. Roy was winding us up in the dressing room. It was live on Sky and Dundee United were near the top. I came out fired up all right. That fired up that I got a yellow card after about ten seconds for my first tackle.

I was trying so hard to make it right for Roy. He was the manager who signed me and I had a lot of respect for him. I felt I owed him with a big performance on a big night.

We kicked off and the ball went to their left back. I ran across and caught him late and was straight in the book. Not a great start.

The night went from bad to worse. Soon we were 3-0 then worse and the writing was on the wall. I'd lost my rag and tackled the same lad, a foreign lad Edison. Eoin Jess played me a ball a bit too long and I just slid in and followed through. F*** it, I was frustrated.

In Scottish football you couldn't raise your feet and Hugh Dallas, the referee, had no choice.

I knew straight away I was off. The lad kicked through my studs and started screaming and rolling about. I just looked up and Dallas ran towards me and gave me a straight red. We were five down at the time.

That was red card number one and I wasn't happy. Their lad had made a meal of it, rolling around like he'd been shot. I called Dallas a f****** joke and stomped off the pitch. As I walked down the tunnel, I punched the corner flag. As I hit it, the flag sprung out of the hole and fell on to the pitch. I was steaming.

After the game, I sat there with a face like thunder. Suddenly there's a knock on the door of the dressing room and it's one of the linesman summoning me and Roy to the referee's office. What have I done now?

Dallas is stood there and says he is reporting me to the Scottish FA for three counts. Not only has he sent me off for the two tackles, he's also sending me off again for foul and abusive language at him and for punching the corner flag. In other words, I was being punished for the equivalent of three red cards. As I'd said earlier, what a f****** joke.

Roy got the sack the next day and I got a six-week ban. My name around Aberdeen was mud. That was effectively the end of my time in Scotland although I didn't realise it at the time. I was banned for six games and hit hard in the pocket. The club fined me two weeks' wages and the Scottish FA did the same.

I couldn't even train properly because I had to do everything on my own. Keith Burkinshaw, the old Tottenham manager, had taken over as caretaker boss with Roy gone and made me train alone in the afternoons. I got the impression that Keith decided I was a bad influence and didn't want me coming anywhere near the other players. I wasn't allowed at the training ground before 1.30 in case any of the lads were still there – I thought he treated me like shit.

Then Alec Miller came in and things had to get better. After the way Keith had been, he was fine with me. At first.

I was a week away from being able to play again when he arrived and Alec picked me for his first game against Motherwell. We won 1-0 and I got the winner. I was made up and so was he, at least that's what I thought.

It was a great comeback for me and the new manager said it was a fresh start. Then he left me out altogether for a big game with Rangers three days later. I'd played well and scored the winning goal but now I wasn't good enough to be in the team for the next game! I couldn't get my head round it and the relationship went rapidly downhill between us.

I just wanted to be playing but I was always a sub. I had permanent splinters in my arse from spending so long sat on the bench. Alec said I wasn't used to playing at a higher level but that wasn't true. He only had to look at my record with Aberdeen to see that.

But the more I moaned, the worse he got. I got the impression he had made up his mind that I was a bad professional and I knew that was it for me in Scotland.

WELCOME HOME

HE STAGGERED TOWARDS ME, the gun in one hand, an empty whisky bottle in the other. I cowered in the corner of the changing room, absolutely shitting myself. The rest of them had bolted the moment he came stumbling in. The first shout of "Where's Windass?" and they were all gone.

I was on my own. I tried the door but it wouldn't budge. I was trapped.

"So you're Windass" he slurred, fixing me with this drunken stare. I nodded and pleaded with him not to kill me. It was the most petrifying moment of my life.

This couldn't be happening to me. One minute we were sat there listening to the manager Mally Shotton go through the itinerary for pre-season and preparing for a trip to Exeter. The next I'm staring down the barrel of a pistol-waving madman.

"I'm going to shoot you, yer bastard," he roared, as the gun shook in his hand. I really thought I was a goner. But all of a sudden, the expression on his face changed. A broad smile broke out as he dropped the weapon and stuck out his hand: "My name's Terry and welcome to Oxford United Football Club."

Bastard. The door flung open and the other lads all piled back in to take the piss, including Mally. So this was my initiation ceremony. My welcome home to English football.

Of course it was a fake gun but it was very, very convincing. Just ask my pants. And when I'd calmed down, I did see the funny side. They did it to all the new guys and it worked a treat every time.

The best one had happened just before my time when big Kevin Francis joined Oxford. Anyone who remembers big Kev will know that he was a 6ft 7in black centre forward who was built like a brick shit house. Nobody dared take any liberties with him. But that didn't get him out of a traditional Oxford welcome. In fact, Terry the "gun man" even made him strip off and chased him naked all round the training pitch!

I have to admit that the whole act was superbly done, though it came to an end the day Paul Tait decided to hit back with a golf club.

Taity, who we'd signed from Birmingham, was so scared that he ran across the training ground and on to the mini golf course next door. There was a bloke putting on the green so Taity runs up to him, grabs the putter and starts swinging it at Terry who's right behind him.

We all ran over shouting that it was a joke and trying to pull him off but not before Taity had landed some big blows. I think he broke poor old matey's arm.

No surprises they scrapped it after that. But it was a very effective way of breaking the ice at a new club and they were a good bunch of lads to be with.

Oxford was my first stop-off south of the border after getting away from Aberdeen. Alec Miller's attitude had made up my mind that I couldn't stay in Scotland and anyway, Josh was coming up to five and was about to start big school which I wanted him to do in England.

A few clubs were showing an interest. Dario Gradi wanted to take me to Crewe but they couldn't afford the asking price and I know Chris Kamara was interested at Stoke. Aberdeen asked about a swap deal for Graham Kavanagh, their midfielder, but Kammy wanted to play us both together and wasn't prepared to let him go. Nothing happened on that front but then Oxford came in.

I'd played with their manager Mally Shotton at Hull for a while and he knew all about me. It was a long way south and I know Helen wanted to get back nearer home, but at least it was the chance to play in England again.

I looked at their league position in the table and they'd finished halfway up the first division the previous season so it seemed a good opportunity. Mally was certainly very keen and he pulled up a few trees to get us there. Oxford paid Aberdeen £475,000 which was a club record by a long way and they also offered me decent wages and a good signing-on fee.

I was under a lot of pressure because of the price tag. Oxford had a few money problems off the field and this was a big gamble to take so I was desperate not to let Mally down.

I was certainly feeling the heat on my debut at Bristol City because it must have been 100 degrees out there. It was the sort of weather to be sat round a Spanish pool with a few beers, not running up and down a football pitch on the opening day of the season.

Mally put me in centre midfield alongside a lad called Martin Gray and we bumped into each other at one stage, allowing them to run through and score. We came in at half-time to a right bollocking from Mally who told me to get my f****** act together. Luckily I did just that in the second half by scoring a beauty from the edge of the box and we drew 2-2.

Just like with Hull, Oxford could not decide where to play me. They thought that midfield was my best position because of my passing ability but I wanted to go up front. Mark Harrison, Mally's number two, said I was a selfish sod looking for personal glory but I think he was more worried about losing me from the middle of the park. But we were struggling to score goals and after another word with Mally, I was played as a striker for a game on Sky against

Portsmouth. I put away a penalty in the first half and then got another late on with half-volley.

It was a great strike to help us win the game and after that I never moved from the position. In fact I couldn't stop scoring and ended up with 18 goals from 38 games, which I thought was a pretty decent effort for a team that ended up being relegated.

We took a couple of real batterings that year and let in seven against Sunderland and Birmingham. It was men against boys at Sunderland who were flying high at the time with Niall Quinn and Kevin Phillips banging in the goals. But the Birmingham game was worse because it was at the Manor Ground where we were usually pretty strong. Despite our position, we were a tough side to beat at home until that day.

It was the last home game before Christmas so Mally made us go out with Santa hats to do the warm-up. The weather was pretty good and the crowd were really up for it so we thought that might create a party atmosphere. Well, at least Birmingham enjoyed themselves.

Seven was my unlucky number that day because I ended up with seven stitches after their centre half Michael Johnson split my ear open when we went up together for a header. At least I managed to score again in the 90th minute. It was 7-0 at the time so didn't really affect the result but I did this daft little dance anyway with a big bandage round my head and it gave our fans something to smile about.

The supporters were brilliant with me that year and on the pitch things were going well personally if not for the team. But it wasn't the same for me away from football because Helen was getting more and more home sick. By this time, she was heavily pregnant with Jordan and was desperate to get back up north and nearer her family.

The real problem was that she had nobody round her during the day and she was stuck indoors while I was off training. We were living in a nice place in Bicester village just off the A43. It was a bit of a culture shock but there was nothing for Helen to do. She had no family or friends about and she was always upset. I'd come home from training in the afternoon and she'd be sat there crying which made it very difficult.

We took in one of the lads, Steve Davis, as a lodger which helped a bit. His family lived in Barnsley so Swede, as we called him, was in a similar position and had got fed up with living in digs and hotels. We gave him our spare room and he paid some rent and having someone else around the house broke the ice with Helen a little bit. But she still had nothing to do and nobody to see during the day.

You know what women are like when they're pregnant, crying all the time over the slightest thing, and she was really far gone with Jordan. We had to get back to the north. I had signed a contract for two and a half years but there was no way we could carry on like that.

Stories appeared on the back pages of the local paper that I wasn't happy with my family life and was looking for a move. Barnsley made an inquiry and John Hendrie offered £250,000 but it was nowhere near enough what Oxford would accept.

Mally made it clear that I would only leave for "mega money" because the last thing they needed in a relegation battle was to lose their star striker. But I had a meeting with Mally and the chairman and took Helen along with me. We explained everything and the chairman promised to take it on board.

Something had to happen and I went to see Mally again. While we were talking in his office, I just burst into tears because I was getting that upset over what the missus was going through. I knew there were clubs in the north after me so I was pleading with him to sell me.

Then I got a phone call from Phil Smith, my agent at the time, saying that Bradford were keen and had offered £950,000. I knew Oxford couldn't afford to turn that down and went in to see Mally again. He'd also been told and knew that nothing he could say would stop the deal being done. My Oxford education was nearly complete.

The last game I played was on a Tuesday night at QPR's Loftus Road. Before we went out, Mally pulled me and tongue-in-cheek suggested that if I tossed it off then he would stop the transfer. At least I think it was tongue-in-cheek. We lost 1-0 to a shitty goal so it was hardly the best way to go. But there were no hard feelings as I walked away.

I had really enjoyed my short time there despite the poor results and the problems at home. My own game had come on and I was scoring goals for fun which is why Bradford, who were pushing hard for promotion to the Premiership, had stepped in.

Oxford didn't really want to sell me to another first division club but they didn't have much choice because they needed the money. And they had made a tidy profit by selling me for double what they had paid eight months earlier.

My goal tally had put me on the map, especially a couple I got in the FA Cup against Chelsea. We had two brilliant games with them in the fourth round and should have knocked them out. They were top of the Premiership at the time and it was real plum draw for Oxford, especially as we were at home. There was a crowd of 9,000 there, which is a full house for the Manor, and it was a fantastic occasion. We were struggling in the league but still fancied ourselves because of the home record. It was live on Sky and we played out of our skins.

I gave us the lead just after half-time, pulling away from Michael Duberry at the near post to score with a header from Joey Beauchamp's corner. Chelsea didn't seem to fancy it and we thought it was going to be our day when Kevin Francis had a great chance for a second with five minutes left. It was a total sitter but big Kev scuffed it wide. And with his frustration at missing such an easy one, he went down the other end in injury time and absolutely poleaxed Gianluca Vialli to give them a penalty. Kev claimed he got a touch and put it out for a throw-in but having seen the video later, there was no way he got near the ball.

Frank Leboeuf stepped up and tucked the penalty in the corner although our young lad in goal, Elliott Jackson, nearly managed to save it. But there was only time to kick off again and the ref blew the final whistle. We had played so well and everyone was absolutely devastated. The dressing room was a morgue even though we'd just drawn with the team top of the league.

Nobody said anything, especially to big Kev. If it had been anybody else launching Vialli then somebody would have smacked him. But there was no shouting or moaning that Kev should have stayed on his f****** feet. Big 6ft 7in Kev got no stick at all – it was just an unfortunate tackle that hadn't come off! He was one scary bloke but a good lad to have in the team. Kev was the ideal partner up front because he'd obviously win everything in the air. He was a great pro but had to give up in the end because of trouble with his knees.

It felt like a defeat but at least we had another crack at Chelsea in the replay. That made the club a few bob and it was a chance to go to Stamford Bridge. Would you believe it we went 1-0 up again when our centre half Phil Gilchrist scored early doors. But it couldn't last and it didn't it after Zola put away a fantastic chip just before half-time. They went 4-1 up before I managed to score again near the end.

My shot was going into the top corner when Dennis Wise pushed it away with his hand. Dennis had already been booked so he was sent-off before I blasted the penalty right down the middle. We'd got beaten but at least I'd scored in both matches against a Premiership side. I didn't realize then but a few months later I would get the chance to be playing against Chelsea again – but this time on level terms in the league.

BIG TIME

THE FIRST TIME I met Paul Jewell was at Center Parcs in Nottingham. We bumped into each other in one of the indoor pools and I recognized him from playing against Bradford in the past. He was a bit worried about getting released as a player and wasn't sure what would happen next. He certainly didn't say anything about coaching at the time.

But a couple of years on, things were different and he was doing a fantastic job at Valley Parade. Bradford took him on as a coach there and when Kammy got the sack, he grabbed his chance as manager with both hands.

Jagger, as everyone knew him, wasn't much older than some of the players. He was only 34 when I went there but you could see that everyone in the dressing room had real respect for him. And the results showed that his methods were working.

My first thought when Bradford came in for me was that it was the move I needed to get back north. It was the chance for me and Helen to get back nearer our families. The league position didn't really come into it until my agent said that the fee had been agreed between the clubs. But when I looked at the table, it was a real no brainer.

From being second from bottom with Oxford and fighting relegation, I was joining a club second from top and in the mix to get into the Premiership. Tough choice, eh!

It was some transformation and the negotiations were easy. I was absolutely delighted Bradford had come in for me and I didn't take much persuading to say yes. You could see that the whole place was buzzing. Walking into the changing room for the first time to meet the lads, I could sense the spirit and high morale that comes from getting results week in, week out.

There were a lot of characters and guys who were good to be around. I'd played against big Darren Moore before and he was a centre half who took no prisoners. Nobody took liberties when he was around. And there were other good players like Stuart McCall in the middle, Jamie Lawrence on the right and Robbie Blake and Lee Mills banging in the goals up front.

I made my debut less than a week after leaving Oxford and couldn't have wished for a bigger game. We were at home to Sunderland, the runaway leaders, and Valley Parade was full. First v second and I couldn't wait.

Peter Beagrie was injured so Blakey played on the left while I partnered Lee Mills in attack. It was a great occasion and I had two or three chances but the ball wouldn't go in.

Sunderland's goalkeeper Thomas Sorensen went off with 20 minutes left after a clash with Millsy and Niall Quinn had to go in goal. But we didn't put him under enough pressure and they won 1-0.

We were all gutted not to get a result but the performance was pretty good and we were still very confident of finishing second. Sunderland were obviously going to win the league and the battle was on for the other automatic spot between us, Ipswich and Birmingham.

The thing I liked was that everybody knew their jobs. We had great organization throughout the team and whether it was the strikers, the midfield, back four or the keeper we all knew what we had to do. There was no messing about with daft formations. Training was virtually the same every day. The methods didn't change – and why should they? As the old saying goes, if it ain't broke, don't fix it and there was nothing wrong with Bradford's results.

Jagger had brought me in as a striker after all the goals I'd been scoring for Oxford and he stood by me as I settled in. The £950,000 price tag was a big one but there were a couple of boys in there who had cost more. Millsy was £1m and Isaiah Rankin cost £1.2m from Arsenal so I didn't feel under any pressure which helped.

The first few weeks were knackering, though, because I was traveling back to Oxford after every game to see Helen. Because she was pregnant, it would have been daft to make her stay in a hotel while we looked for a new house so every week I'd bomb down the motorway.

I was sharing the same hotel as Lee Sharpe, who had signed for Bradford from Sampdoria. You know what Sharpey's like and it was a pretty social occasion with the odd beer here or there. I'm sure Jagger must have known about it but he didn't let on.

It looked like we would hold our nerve and hang on to second place. Birmingham had fallen away and it was a straight dogfight between us and Ipswich with just two games to go.

Our final home game was at home to Oxford, my old club. They needed the points just as much but for very different reasons at the other end of the table. The away fans gave me a load of hammer. You greedy bastard and all that. I just laughed it off. But the result wasn't so funny.

Jagger said afterwards that he felt people assumed that we just had to turn up to win. And football doesn't work like that. Oxford fought for their lives and hung on for a 0-0 draw. You'd have thought they'd won promotion from the reaction of their supporters afterwards but they'd certainly got one over me.

We should still have won it because there were plenty of chances.

The best one went begging five minutes from the end and I thought it had cost us promotion. I put in a cross for Stuart McCall which on any other day he would have buried with his eyes shut. But this time his header went over the bar. We couldn't believe it and it was difficult doing the usual lap of honour after the final whistle. The lads wanted to thank the fans for their support but you couldn't help feeling that we'd let ourselves down.

But we still had one more chance although it wasn't going to be easy. Our last game was away to Wolves and they needed the points as well to nick into the play-offs. We knew it was going to be a brilliant atmosphere at Molineux and the week before really dragged.

There was massive interest from the media in the build-up so Jagger decided to take us away for a few days to a hotel where we could play a bit of golf and practise without all the cameras on us.

Jagger had played me in most of the games but I just sensed that I wasn't in the side for Sunday. So when he pulled me with the bad news, I wasn't really that surprised. I was gutted to be on the bench but I could see his reasons why. You couldn't drop Millsy our top scorer and he wanted to play Robbie Blake up with him because he'd done well against Wolves earlier in the season. It was the biggest match of my life and I was one of the subs along with Sharpey and Gordon Watson.

There were thousands of Bradford fans who had made the trip and the noise was brilliant. But it couldn't have started any worse for us when Flo put Wolves in front early on.

Some teams would have panicked but everyone was still confident. It was only a matter of time before we came back and got promoted.

Sure enough, Millsy scored his 25th of the season with a great goal and Beags made it 2-1 before half-time. We were that close but Jagger made sure everyone stayed calm and his team talk at the break was all about finishing the job and not letting our guard down.

Nobody was letting up and when Blakey got the third, we were virtually there. Or so it seemed.

We got a penalty but Beags missed it and then Paul Simpson pulled one back for them. The tension was getting unbearable. It was worse being on the sidelines not being able to do anything about it so I was relieved when Jagger finally sent me on. There was only about ten minutes to go and I went into centre midfield with Sharpey wide on the left. Wolves were pushing for an equalizer and were getting closer and closer. Then they won a free-kick in a really dangerous position.

We knew how good Simpson can be from a set-piece and feared the worst. Gary Walsh, our keeper, lined up the wall and I was on the end. But none of us could do anything about it as Simpson bent the ball round the wall. As I turned my head to watch, I was convinced the ball was going in. Walshy was stood still, he hadn't even tried to dive because there was no chance of reaching it. We were f*****.

But somehow the ball smacked against the inside of the post and bounced straight back into his arms. And that was the point when we all knew that this really was going to be our day.

The stoppage time seemed to take forever and whenever one of us got the ball, we'd just launch it as long and as far as we could up the pitch and away from our goal. Then the referee Chris Foy blew his whistle and the world went mad. Gary Walsh and Darren Moore fell to the floor and I dived on top of them, everywhere the lads were going ballistic. It's hard to find the words to describe how we felt at that moment. It was like waking up and finding your dream was real.

Nobody could believe it but we were in the Premier League. Bradford had done it. One minute I'd nearly been relegated with Oxford, now I was in a team looking forward to playing against Man United, Liverpool and Arsenal every week!

The changing room was carnage. I was squashed in a single bath with Beags and a bottle of champagne, necking it back in huge gulps.

There was champagne and cans of beer everywhere. The emotion was so much we were all pissed up within an hour. Reporters and camera crews were getting loads of interviews and there was alcohol spraying everyone. It was just an unbelievable scene.

I don't think we came out the changing room for about two and a half hours because there was so much going on. When we did, everyone was worse for wear and the real party hadn't even started.

We got back on the bus to get stuck into some more beer on the way home. As the gaffer got on, he announced that we would all be getting a promotion bonus. And because of that, he said, all debts from the card schools will be wiped out. You should have seen Beags' face.

We used to play three-card brag and a few of the lads owed a bit of money. I used to play with Beags, Jags, John Dreyer, Blakey and Terry Yorath and Beags reckoned Blakey owed him about £1,200. So he wasn't amused when Jagger announced that all bets were off!

But it didn't take Beags long to cheer up again as the beer kept flowing on the way home.

Nobody bothered getting any cards out because there was some serious celebrating to do. And it got even better when the gaffer's phone rang to say that the chairman had organized a party for us when we got back to Valley Parade. Everyone was on their mobiles phoning their wives and girlfriends and sorting out baby sitters because it was going to be a very long night.

It's about two and a half hours from Wolves to Bradford so you can imagine the state we were in as the coach pulled up among all the fans waiting to see us. We all got off the bus with cans in our hand. That was when Stuart did his famous fall off a car bonnet – and not spilling a drop of his open beer! It's a moment that nobody ever forgets and just sums up the day.

Alan Jackson, our kitman at the time, told us to leave all the clothes, golf clubs and stuff on the bus and we piled into the party upstairs. It went on all night and you couldn't get Beags and Stuart off the karaoke. Beags' wife was also belting it out and all of them thought they could sing. But there was that much beer being drunk that nobody was complaining.

It had been a great day but the celebrations went on for a few weeks after that.

Paul took us all to Magaluf for five days which was an experience and a half. All the squad were there except for Beags. His missus had put her foot down and wouldn't let him go so he got plenty of stick.

We had some big drinkers in the side. Blokes like Ashley Westwood, Jamie Lawrence and Sharpey could put a few away and we all came back with alcoholic poisoning. We'd be round the pool every day having a drink and then hit the town in the evening. Big Darren Moore was absolutely brilliant for keeping everyone together on our nights out. He didn't drink that much so he was our Mr T, sniffing out trouble.

One day we were sat outside a bar when the Aston Villa boss John Gregory walked by. Seeing us all sat there with our beers, he started taking the piss and someone heard him say "Bradford City, who are they?" Darren got a whisper of this and we thought he was going to throttle Gregory but managed to calm down. John doesn't know how lucky he was.

But it was a great trip to finish off a great season and just what we all needed to unwind. My first year back in England couldn't have gone much better and now I had my first taste of the Premiership to look forward to.

I knew how tough it was going to be. All the experts were writing off Bradford even before the fixtures came out, saying that we'd have no chance of staying up. It was going to be a massive job but not impossible. But we had to be performing at our very best to hope to pull it off.

I wanted to make sure I was in the best possible shape for playing against all the top players. So the moment I got back from Magaluf, I got into training. There was no summer holiday that year because it was so important I was fully fit and fired up. I'd go out running every single day, pegging it up and down the road. All I could see in front of me was the bright lights of the Premiership and nothing was going to hold me back.

I felt unbelievable when we came back in for pre-season. On the first day of training, we were sent on two-milers as quick as we could go and I was one of the first to finish along with Andy O'Brien.

At the end of the session, Stuart sat us all down on the grass for a meeting. He said he'd been in to see the chairman as captain and they'd drawn up a list of bonuses for us in the Premiership. It's a fiver for a corner and tenner for a shot …

MISSION IMPOSSIBLE

DEAN WINDASS, PREMIERSHIP PLAYER. It sounded brilliant. This was my dream since the moment I'd started kicking a football. I was mixing it with the top players in the top league. Not for one-off cup games but week in, week out testing my skills against some of the best in the world.

I had to keep pinching myself. Every run I went on that summer all I could picture was the names that Bradford would be up against – Manchester United, Arsenal, Liverpool, Chelsea. I couldn't wait for the fixture list to come out. The day it did I felt like a kid on Christmas morning. Our first game was away to Middlesbrough – our last at home to Liverpool. Little did anyone know how big a match that was going to be.

Everyone had written us off, of course. The moment the final whistle had gone at Wolves, I bet there were people running to the bookies to back us to go straight back down. All the experts gave us no chance. Rodney Marsh used to slaughter us every week on Soccer Saturday on Sky. If we somehow managed to stay up, he said, "I'll shave my head for charity" …

Paul Jewell wasn't getting carried away. He came out and said our main aim was to finish fourth from bottom. If we do that then it was mission accomplished. It didn't sound like much of a goal but when you consider what we were going to be up against, it was a tough enough one. We didn't kid ourselves. We knew that it was all about survival and avoiding relegation. Staying up for us would be like winning the league for Man United.

We expected to get dumped 3-0 or 4-0 along the way. When you think what we'd be up against, there were going to be days when the opposition looked unstoppable. If the top teams are on top of their game then anyone will struggle to hold them. But it was how we responded to those beatings that would show whether we had a chance or not. The gaffer kept ramming it in to us that it's how we bounced back to defeats that was crucial. If we lose by three or four, then make sure it doesn't happen again the following week. And to be fair, I can't recall us getting done too many times on the bounce by that margin.

We had signed some players with Premiership experience, the likes of David Wetherall from Leeds and Dean Saunders. Blimey, I thought, we're getting a big club now signing players like that. That was when it really start to sink in that we were in the big time.

It was Deano, the other Deano, who got us off to a dream start at the Riverside. He came on for me just before the end and then scored the only goal in the last minute when he slipped the ball under Mark Schwarzer.

When he celebrated, everyone was holding his back while he pretended to walk with a stick like an old man. We'd already been slagged off as Dad's Army by the press and this was our way of answering back.

We were ready to prove a few people wrong.

Paul Gascoigne was playing for Middlesbrough that day and Jagger had decided to give Andy O'Brien the job of man-marking him. It was going to be hard enough anyway but somehow the press had got wind of it and it had leaked out in the papers the day before.

We were in the tunnel waiting to go out and everyone was nervous. Then Gazza shouts out to OB to come over. "I'm over here, come and stand here" and giving it all that.

But OB didn't crack and went on to do his job really well. He had passed his first big test and so had we. It was a special welcome to the Premier League. It was a real bonus to get three points on the road like that because our best chance was to do well at home. We had to make Valley Parade a fortress.

We knew it wasn't just a case of taking points off the teams in and around the bottom. We had to upset some of the big boys and make coming to Bradford as uncomfortable as possible. We'd get nothing from them at Highbury, Old Trafford and Anfield but at Valley Parade there was always a chance. And it worked with results at home against Arsenal, Chelsea and Tottenham.

Valley Parade is not a bad ground but the facilities for the players are not the best. But that worked to our advantage when the big hitters were in town. We played Arsenal and you could see the likes of Petit and Ljungberg looking round this shitty little changing room and wondering "what the f*** are we doing here?"

That must have been playing on their minds when we went out there and beat them 2-1. I scored a free-kick and Dean Saunders got the winner. You could see that Arsenal weren't used to that environment and it must have thrown them out of their usual game. Of course it was completely different when we went down to Highbury.

Jagger's team talk before the game was all about keeping it tight and not conceding in the first 20 minutes. If we can get that far and it's still 0-0 then maybe we've got a chance.

And whatever you do, he said, do not give away any free-kicks around the box. So what happens? Arsenal get a free-kick and Vieira scores from it with a header. And within 15 minutes, they are 2-0 up and taking the piss.

It could have been seven or eight that day. In fact, they could have won 10-0 and we wouldn't have complained. Luckily Gary Walsh was absolutely outstanding in our goal. Some of the saves he pulled off were just incredible and somehow they didn't score again. We were quite happy to come away with only losing 2-0.

Arsenal were on a different level. Paul was watching their bench and at one point Pat Rice got up to give somebody a bollocking. But Arsene Wenger just tapped him on the shoulder, telling him to sit down and let them get on with it. There was hardly any coaching involved because they were such good players.

I was playing on the right of a midfield three along with Stuart McCall and Neil Redfearn. Unfortunately Thierry Henry was wide left for them. It wasn't a lot of fun having the job of trying to chase him back all the time and still attempt to get in their box and push forward when we managed to get the ball.

After an hour or so the substitution board came up and number 14, Henry's number, was on it. Thank f*** for that, my legs had totally gone. But who came on instead? Only Marc f****** Overmars, who was even quicker! I had nothing left but kept going on adrenaline alone. This was why I did all that running every day in the summer holidays. You had to be so physically fit or these top players would just kill you.

Liverpool away was another memorable day because it was live on Sky on a Monday night. The atmosphere was brilliant and when I scored early on it was the highlight of my career. The ball came in from Lee Mills, though I'm not sure if he dropped it off to me or it was a bad touch. But I dummied it and then hit a half-volley sweet as a nut. Sander Westerveld dived but got nowhere near it and I'd scored in front of the Kop to put little Bradford City 1-0 up at Liverpool.

They couldn't believe it and before anyone had really recovered, we should have had another. Dean Saunders broke down the left and crossed for Neil Redfearn who put his header over the bar. It was a sitter especially for Neil who was a good finisher for a midfield player and had scored a few for Barnsley in the Premier League before. But this time he put it into the Kop instead of the back of the net and our chance of causing the biggest shock of the season had gone with it.

All right, I'm not saying we would definitely have won after going 2-0 up. But at least we'd have stood a genuine chance of holding on. We all knew what was coming next. Having blown it at one end, we were punished straight away at the other through Titi Camara. Then Jamie Redknapp got a penalty before half-time and Liverpool went on to win 3-1.

But it was still a great moment for me to score at Anfield, especially at the Kop end.

Not that my goal is the thing most people remember about me from that game. There was a funnier incident that often gets played back on Sky when I accidentally smacked ref Jeff Winter with the ball.

It was just after he'd given them the penalty. Andy O'Brien had got nutmegged by Camara who'd gone down easily and they got the decision. We were disputing the penalty and I just blasted the ball away in frustration. Unfortunately it flew straight at the ref and smacked him right on the earpiece on the side of his head. Jeff was staggering about because it had been really travelling.

F****** hell, I thought, he's going to think I've done that on purpose and I'll be off. Jeff didn't know what had happened at first but when he came to his senses, he went over to Michael Owen, who was standing close by, to find out who the culprit had been.

By this point I was nowhere to be seen. I'd feared the worst and decided the best thing was to try and hide in the middle with everyone else. Luckily Jeff didn't take it any further because he couldn't be sure if it was me or not. But Sky knew, of course, and asked me after the game if I'd meant to do it. Course not, I said, because if I'd been deliberately aiming at him I would have missed …

Jeff was quality about it later but that's the kind of bloke he is. He's a big Middlesbrough fan and ironically when I joined Boro a bit later we became good friends. But he was that rare breed of ref who didn't mind a bit of banter and showed a lot of commonsense. He wasn't like one of these robots you see everywhere. If you had a go at him, he'd have a pop straight back. Shut the f*** up Windass, I'm reffing this game not you. There was no messing about but you knew exactly where you stood. And that's all you can ask from the referee.

Unfortunately that wasn't the case with every official we had in the Premiership and I'm sure we missed out on key decisions because we weren't one of the big boys. We were little Bradford City, just there for the year, so what did it matter?

We played Man United at Old Trafford and were hanging on for 0-0 with 74 minutes gone. Then Gary Neville went right through the back of me in their penalty area. It had to be a penalty and Jagger was screaming for the foul on the touchline. But nothing was given and, of course, they scored from their next attack.

Maybe at Valley Parade we might have got the decision. But away from home there was no chance, especially at somewhere like that.

There were quite a few of us in the squad who were new to the Premier League and we had to learn fast. We couldn't afford to give the ball away cheaply or you wouldn't see it again.

In the home game with United, we couldn't get possession back and I was getting pissed off chasing all the time. David Beckham had it just outside our box and I kicked him. He got straight back up and bent the free-kick over our wall and in the top corner. The gaffer hammered me about it afterwards. What was I doing kicking the best free-kick taker in the world? I might as well have given them the goal.

We were down the bottom, as everyone had expected, but were fighting hard. Nobody was going to give it up while we still had a chance.

It looked good when we went to West Ham and I put us one up early on. But none of us knew what was going to follow. It was more like a Sunday League game than the Premiership. By half-time they had leveled it at 2-2 but Jamie Lawrence scored twice in the six minutes after the break and we looked to be cruising it.

It should have been game over but this is Bradford City we're talking about. Di Canio, who had sat down in the centre circle in a sulk for some reason, got back up and scored. Then they equalized to make it 4-4 before Frank Lampard smashed in a left-foot shot right at the end to win it.

Everything kicked off in our dressing room with a ruck between Stuart McCall and Dean Saunders. Stuart was laying into him for being selfish and wasting a great chance to have made it 5-2. Dean had gone through on the right and I was backing up play and there for a simple tap-in in the middle if he'd passed it. But instead, he went for glory himself and tried a shot with the outside of right foot which hit the post. Stuart was furious about it and was right in Dean's face, hammering him. Dean wouldn't back down and told him: Shut it, you prick. Then it all went off.

One thing Stuart didn't like was people calling him a prick and Dean said it a couple of times. They were at each other's throats and everyone had to jump in the middle. It was like the fight at the OK Corral.

We were all gutted about losing the game. How could you score four goals away from home in the Premiership and end up with nothing to show for it? The chairman had a go at Jagger afterwards for his tactics. We had John Dreyer, a centre half, on the bench and we'd not brought him on when West Ham were pouring forward.

That was the start of the problems between Richmond and Paul Jewell although, at the time, we were too pissed off with the long coach journey home to worry about anything else.

But like most rucks in the dressing room, it quickly blew over between Stuart and Dean. It was heat of the moment stuff because we were annoyed and you couldn't stay mad at Dean Saunders for long. He was the joker in the squad and always made sure he had the last say. He would rattle off story after story and take people off brilliantly and have us in fits with his impressions.

He would mimic some of the managers he'd played under like Cloughy, Frank Clark and I remember him taking Terry Yorath off one day – and Taff was stood in the doorway behind him listening to every word. Even he had to admit that Dean was very good. Dean would hammer Robbie Blake day after day, usually about his clothes. He was always chasing Blakey up for money after he'd lost at cards.

We all knew Dean had a bob or two from his career and Blakey would ask him why he needed the cash so urgently. "I need £30 or £40 for petrol so I can drive from my front door to the gate!"

Jorge Cadete, a Portuguese lad who had done well at Celtic, came in on loan and Dean was soon ripping in to him. I remembered Jorge from my days at Aberdeen when he used to bang in 30 goals a season in Scotland. But he was always injured or complaining about knocks. Every day he'd have an ice pack on some part of his leg or other and Dean reckoned he had his own personal supply flown in from home.

But Dean would take the piss out of the management just as much as the other players. Once Billy Brown, the assistant manager when Jim Jefferies took over, collared Dean to tell him that Dundee United were interested in him. "Interested in me to do what?" Dean replied. "To buy the club?" This was right in front of the lads and we all burst out laughing. "I'm only 36 years old," he said. "Why do I want to play in Scotland yet?"

But Dean was a great lad and typical of the characters we had in that dressing room. Even though he was the worst trainer I've ever seen. He used to slag people off on the training ground and moan at everything. But when he went out on a match day, he was brilliant and I loved playing up front with him. Even at that age, he was still making great runs and was a really intelligent forward. You could see why Paul brought him in.

If losing 5-4 at West Ham wasn't mad enough, we had another amazing game when we played Derby at Valley Parade. It was Good Friday and a massive match for both of us because we were in the bottom three and they were only just above.

Jagger decided to push David Wetherall up from centre half to centre forward to play alongside me so they could hit the diagonal balls and use him as a targetman. It worked a treat and Wethers did the job really well, winning a lot of crosses and nodding them down for me. All I had to do was get on the end of his headers and put them away.

It was my first Premiership hat-trick and another great day for me personally. But again it was so frustrating for the team as Derby kept coming back. Craig Burley got a couple for them and it ended up as a 4-4 draw which wasn't much good to either team.

Paul watched the highlights later and reckoned we defended like the Dog and Duck with the goals we conceded. But I watch the match back again now when the Premiership Years come on Sky and it's still very special. It was also the first hat-trick ball in my Bradford collection.

But time was ticking away for us. Games were running out and we knew that our trip to Sunderland on the following Monday was a must-win. Wimbledon were collapsing all the time and we still had to play them at Valley Parade. But we needed the three points from the Stadium of Light first if we were going to be able to put them under real pressure at our place.

There was a massive crowd at Sunderland but we were quite confident. They were safely mid-table and had nothing to play for so we definitely wanted it the most. And the lad who scored our winning goal that day will never let anyone forget it. John Dreyer, or Tumble as he was known, didn't get many so this was pretty special.

Beags made the cross and Tumble headed it home although Dean Saunders tried to claim the goal by saying it went in off his leg. The two of them were still arguing like f*** about it for the next week in training but whoever got the last touch, it was a huge moment for us. Tumble got hammered for his celebrations afterwards when the lads saw it again on the TV.

He ran off waving his arms and as we all piled on him, you could lip-read him shouting "we're still in there, we're still in there." But he was right. We were still in there and Wimbledon must have been shitting it.

It was still win or bust for us when we played them. The Dons had been dropping like a stone but if they took anything from Valley Parade, we'd be left with too much to do in the last couple of games. We knew it was going to be a tense afternoon. And we soon found out just how tense when it went off in the tunnel before we had even got on the pitch.

Big John Hartson was pacing up and down before we came out of the changing room. I looked at him and he had this mad look in his eyes as if he was that pumped up he was in a trance.

Stuart left the room first as captain and, as usual, I hung back to go out as the last man. Suddenly there was all this shouting and shoving coming from outside. The two captains had clashed near the referee's room and John kneed Stuart in the bollocks. He was trying to grab him by the throat at the same time but Wayne Jacobs got involved and started throwing punches back.

Wayne is a born again Christian but he knows how to handle himself and he waded in firing lefts and rights like Lennox Lewis to get Hartson away from Stuart before the officials could sort it out. I was watching all this from the back because the tunnel was too narrow to move. Mind you, Wimbledon had some big bastards in their team so I was quite happy not to be caught up in it.

John Hartson was so fired up it was unbelievable. Jeff Winter was the ref again and he threatened to book him in the tunnel if he didn't calm down but you could see that Hartson was out of control.

The game went perfectly for us after Jason Euell missed a great chance early on. After that, Wimbledon did nothing and we coasted to a 3-0 win. I got the third goal and Hartson was sent off after 50 minutes for elbowing OB. Nobody was surprised because of the way he'd gone on in the tunnel.

I bumped into him after the game and asked what all that had been about. I understand Vinnie Jones had told him to take out Bradford's big hitter and the rest of us would crumble. He thought Stuart was our main man and if we saw him getting battered like that, we wouldn't want to know afterwards.

But Stuart never backed down and when Wayne and everybody else got involved, Hartson realized that we were made of solid stuff. Great advice, Vinnie. Hartson let his team down by getting sent off and they rolled over easily.

So the Great Escape was still on – and came down to the final match of the season. We just had to do better than Wimbledon in our last game and we'd survive. It sounds simple written down like that. And they had to play Southampton at The Dell, which was never an easy place for anyone to go. But we were up against Liverpool, who needed it just as much.

We were playing for our Premiership lives but they had to win as well to get into the Champions' League. If they cocked it up, Leeds would take fourth spot instead – it was the first time ever Bradford City fans wanted to do Leeds United a favour.

But we had the big advantage of being at home and the atmosphere at Valley Parade was unbelievable. It was boiling hot as well as we prepared for the biggest match of our lives.

This was bigger than Wolves the year before. This was bigger than anything. Bradford City's survival in the Premiership rested on the next 90 minutes.

We were excited but nobody was nervous. We'd seen their team line-up, with the likes of Jamie Redknapp playing on the left, and thought we could win. Yes, they had some good players but they weren't world beaters and we fancied ourselves against anyone at home.

To be honest, the game is still a bit of a blur. Gunnar Halle, our right back, crossed from a free-kick and Wethers produced a great header that thumped past Westerveld. Everyone went mad and chased Dave across the pitch. He's never been the quickest and I don't know where he got the speed from that day as he ran off to celebrate.

Liverpool had chances to come back but we were still 1-0 up into the second half when there was this massive noise ringing round the ground. The hairs on the back of my neck were standing up. What's going on? I thought it might have been a bomb scare or something stupid but it was the fans cheering the news that Southampton had taken the lead against Wimbledon.

Then they got a second goal which meant a draw would be good enough for us. But we'd gone into the game with the attitude that only a win would do and nobody was taking any chances.

There were a couple of minutes left when we cleared a Liverpool corner and Wethers picked me out on the halfway line. The instructions from the sidelines were to waste time by running the ball into the corner. But I was physically and mentally knackered. There was nothing left in my legs. I couldn't have run if I'd wanted to.

I spotted their keeper off his line. He'd come up for the corner and was still on his way back. So I decided to do a David Beckham and shoot from the halfway line. Paul told me later that he was about to give me a right bollocking to his assistant Terry Yorath. But he got as far as "what the f*** has he...." when Westerveld just managed to stretch enough to tip it over the bar.

Jagger was initially angry that I'd just give them the ball back by trying a stupid shot from miles out. But I'd nearly scored and won us a corner instead!

We played out the last couple of minutes and by the time the ref blew his whistle, there were fans swarming all over the pitch. It was absolute mayhem. We are staying up, we are staying up. The chant got louder and louder and it sounded f****** brilliant. Bradford City had proved all the experts and the pundits wrong – we were staying up. F*** the lot of them.

This was the moment we'd all worked so hard for. All that running and fitness work the previous summer had paid off. Everyone had got their reward. It was more than one game, this was a season of bloody hard work. We'd come through so many ups and downs and then to beat Liverpool at home was the perfect way to go out.

The Premiership was a totally different world to anything I had experienced before. And there were so many people queuing up to tell us that we didn't belong there. But those little digs and snide comments gave us an extra oomph. They didn't just piss you off but made you even more determined to shove those words where the sun doesn't shine. The only way to do that was by performing on the pitch.

Rodney Marsh was hammering us week in, week out on Soccer Saturday. But, fair play to him, he had the bottle to have his head shaved for charity and even did it on the pitch before one of our home games.

You expect some stick on the TV and in the papers but there were players having a go as well. The Derby defender Spencer Prior slaughtered us and reckoned we were the worst Premiership team ever – and we'd beaten them 1-0!

We also learned that everyone had to be careful what they said to the press. The papers were always looking to catch you out and blowing your quotes out of all proportion so it made a better headline. I won't deny that I've always liked talking to the media but I got caught out when we went to Chelsea.

In the days leading up to the game, Jagger had told us not to say anything out of turn. If we said something stupid and they twisted it in the London press, then we'd be writing Chelsea's team talk for them.

Most of the reporters wanted to talk to me because I'd played against them the previous year with Oxford in the FA Cup and nearly won. They asked what Oxford had done to frighten Chelsea and how we should approach this game. I remembered Paul's warning not to be controversial and just said something about getting in their faces and not giving good players the chance to get the ball down and play round us. Nothing wrong with that, I thought.

The morning of the game I came down for breakfast in our hotel and Jagger was sat there with the paper and a face like thunder. He calls me over and throws The Sun at me. You couldn't miss the headline: Windass blasts Southern Softies.

There was a big article saying that I reckoned we'd turn over Chelsea because they were worried about a physical game and couldn't handle the rough stuff. I tried to explain to Paul that I never meant it like that but the whole story had killed me. I found out later that Chelsea had pinned it up – I'd done their team talk all right. Gianfranco Zola was outstanding and they ran rings round us. There was nothing soft about their performance. I'd learned the hard way that in the Premiership you not only had to be careful what you did on the field but what you said off it.

BIG TIME BRADFORD

HOW MUCH? Forty two f****** grand a week to play for Bradford? That was more than the rest of us were getting put together. Nice work if you can get it.

None of us knew that Benito Carbone was on the way. The chairman loved all the suspense and all he'd say was that there was going to be a signing on the way, a big signing. He wouldn't tell any of the players who it was. We were as much in the dark as the supporters about this mystery top man.

Geoffrey Richmond loved it that way. He always wanted to be the centre of attention – if he was a piece of chocolate, he'd have ate himself. He kept this story quiet for a couple of days and then I saw the mad scenes on the local news. There was Geoffrey with Beni and several hundred fans in this press conference at the club. At first, I was convinced we'd signed a wrong 'un. He hadn't got the best reputation in the world, falling out with Sheffield Wednesday and going AWOL with Aston Villa.

There was the time he was left out of the team to play at Southampton and rather than watch the game in the stand, he pissed off in a taxi for the nearest airport. He didn't sound like the sort of character we wanted in our situation. We'd had a brilliant spirit in the dressing room for the past two seasons and that had played a massive part in our success. If you put in someone like that who wouldn't mix, then how would it affect things?

We heard the rumours about his wages like everyone else. Players talk about what people are on, especially in the Premier League, and we couldn't believe our ears at the figure he was meant to be getting. You've worked your arse off all these years to get to the top and all of a sudden, someone comes in and takes all the money.

But they were only rumours at that stage, not facts. Nobody seriously believed he was on £40,000-£42,000 a week – at least, not at first.

Not only was he on mega money but the club were also giving him an £800,000 house in Leeds. There was another story that his son was allergic to the carpets when they moved in – so Bradford paid for them to be replaced with wooden flooring. Basically, whatever Beni wanted, they gave it to him. He blew the wage structure right open.

He was the chairman's signing, without a doubt, and had his total backing. Beni even brought in his own fitness trainer from Italy because he didn't think we were training hard enough. Geoffrey was happy to do that. In the space of a couple of months, the club had changed completely.

Paul Jewell had gone off to Sheffield Wednesday after his bust-up with Geoffrey, who was virtually running the show now. Paul going came as a massive shock and I only found out when I popped into the club just before pre-season. Chris Hutchings, the first-team coach, was in the car park and he told me the news. The first thing I wanted to know was who would replace him. "Me," said Hutch.

He'd been at the club a few years and, like he'd done with Paul, Geoffrey decided to appoint from within. I suppose his thinking was that Hutch knew all the players and the system we used so it was no big risk. It was a brilliant chance for Hutch, his first managerial job at a Premier League club. But it meant that Geoffrey could effectively make all the decisions because his manager didn't want to rock the boat.

The summer of 2000 was what Geoffrey later called his "six weeks of madness" when he suddenly brought in all these players on massive wages. I think he must have seen us as a top-ten team now rather than one that had just beaten the drop. I'm sure that none of our signings that year were made by the manager. He didn't seem to have much say in anything. I don't think he wanted Beni but had no choice about it.

Hutch only had us for a week in pre-season before we were in the Intertoto Cup. Paul thought it was a waste of time and didn't want to be involved but the chairman was adamant we took part – which was probably another reason behind their split.

Hutch brought in someone I knew very well to help him. Mally Shotton, the sergeant major, was his number two so this was the third club we'd been at together. They were the good cop, bad cop combination because Hutch was a nice person. Maybe a bit too nice and he was probably happier as the second hand rather than the number one.

But he'd been given this chance and we got a result for him in the first match away in Lithuania. It was a shit hole place to play in but the supporters loved it, spending their time going into the local brothels where it was 50p a pint and £3 a shag. We were trying to prepare for a serious game and they were all out getting blathered.

We hardly had any players at the time so the team was full up with young lads and first-year apprentices. But we still won the game and I scored with a free-kick so everyone was happy.

The trip home was good, too, because they put on a private jet for the players and supporters to fly back together. It was one of those you expect to see some famous singer like Robbie Williams using because it had a big round settee in the middle. We all had a few

Here I am receiving my sportsman of the year award for my dad's team - Ross Group. I was their number one supporter and mascot. Terry Kent, then landlord of the Phoenix Club in Hull, is handing me the plaque. The man on the mic was the team manager Freddy 'Oggy'.

The all-conquering Francis Askew school team with football-mad teacher Dougie Fairlow.

Gipsyville boys

Hull boys

Francis
Askew
school
team

Francis
Askew
U11s

Name: Dean WINDASS   Report for: Summer 1981

Subject	Rating	
English	C D	Dean tries hard, usually and does produced some quite good work	JH
Mathematics	D	One track mind and its not maths. I hope he will not give to regret it.	BS
Tech. Subjects	C D+	Careless work for 'showing little effort	
Sciences	C D	Some improvement in attitude and results	
Domestic Subjects			
Social Studies			
Geog.	C C	Has good ideas when he concentrate	SS
History	C	Fairly good exam result	JM
Music	C+ C+	Quite good.	
Mod. Language			
Art/Craft	B C+	Dean has some ability but lacks confidence. He gives up far too early and becomes frustrated	DG
Religious Education	C	Some good work done	
Physical Education	B+	Getting to like his own way too much.	DS

Attendance: 156 / 158

Punctuality: Good.

Conduct

Good. Has slipped into some bad habits lately.

Notable Performances and Achievements   A.A. 2 ✱

U.13 Cricket 1st XI   Under 12 Soccer Team

Hockey 1st XI   1 merit   City boys U.13, U.12 Captains.

Athletics Team   School Rep. Penalty Comp. 3 ✱ Printfield

Form Teacher's Comments   Dean is still not making the most of his time in school. There can be no doubt of his abilities, but unless he puts in the work then we might never see his grades reflect them.

Signature: Sergeant Jardine

Head Teacher's Comments   I do wish Dean would work as hard in school as he seems to do on the football field - then he would surprise us all.

Signature: H.H. Speller

This to is certify that I have read this report:

D. Windrass.....Parent

Here I am aged about 11 walking off the pitch after a match. The blond lad playing with his fingers is Sean Foster, my best mate from school. The other lad is Mike Smith - who's married to my wife Helen's twin sister Debbie.

Another trophy - can't remember what it was for though. I think the lady presenting it was a local councillor called Mrs Ellis.

This is me with Jason Able and the Rugby League Challenge Cup. Jason's uncle, Mick Harrison, played for Hull.

Finally made it. Me signing pro forms for Hull alongside Terry Dolan.

AGAINST ALL HODS: Dean Windass has made it in professional soccer at the second attempt and has hung up his hod for good - see page four.

The building site was welcome relief from frozen peas and definitely helped build up my strength.

This 1990's tiger striped Hull City kit regularly makes it into the 'top ten worst kits' lists. I think I look rather good in it.

Left: Me and Helen on our wedding day outside Beverley Registry Office.

Right: Like father like son - Josh the Tiger.

Above: Another day, another bollocking.

Opposite page: I've worked on the goal celebrations -
they're certainly more elaborate these days.

Left: 'I'm free!'

Gazza - football genius and someone I've always looked up to.
I was told to man-mark him. He got a hat-trick that day.

What's that? "F****** English Bastard!"

Oxford had just drawn in the cup against the Premiership leaders, but we were gutted. We should have won. FA Cup, Fourth Round, Oxford United v Chelsea 25/1/99.

After costing Bradford £950,000, I had a lot to prove.

drinks and a good craic and nobody wanted to get off when we got back to Leeds/Bradford airport.

But Beni's arrival showed how ambitious the club had become. He would come into training every day in a suit. While the rest of us turned up in t-shirt and jeans, he'd be there all dolled up as if he was going to a night club.

Beni was professional in everything he did and had a great attitude to work. He was a very nice man although I never socialised with him. If I went out drinking, it would be with the usual suspects who lived local – Sharpey, Jamie Lawrence and Ashley Westwood. You couldn't get Beni out for a few beers.

But on the pitch we were both on the same wavelength. I was happy to take the battering from the opposition centre halves and he'd play round the front of us. We had a great understanding and he was a top quality player all right.

I'm not sure if he was worth the money in our situation but you can't blame Beni for that. If someone throws you £42,000 a week you're not going to turn round and say that's too much. Every supporter in the country would take the cash if they got that chance. I know I would.

It was Geoffrey's decision to pay silly money so he was the one to blame, not Beni. He was spot on every day and did everything 100 per cent. Although he didn't mix much, he was good around the training ground and didn't act the big-time Charlie. He was temperamental like a lot of foreign players and some things would upset him but he never let it affect his work.

Beni must have been homesick because he would never go to eat with the lads. Instead he'd be at the local pizza restaurant every day – every afternoon, every night eating pasta and all the Italian food. You don't really know what goes on outside the club but he was a family man. He had a tattoo of the face of his wife right near his groin!

But Beni wasn't the only big name and two weeks later Dan Petrescu arrived from Chelsea. He looked a good signing with his record playing in the Premier League as well as the World Cup for Romania. I'd watched him a lot on TV and thought he would make a real difference to us. Unfortunately it didn't work out great for Dan but in the time he was at Bradford, he certainly changed my lifestyle.

I thought he was an unbelievable pro, always eating and drinking the right things and he educated me a hell of a lot about how to maintain your peak fitness. He taught me how to prepare properly for games, what to do, what to eat, it was a different world. He'd bring in digestive biscuits before games and would show me all these stretches he would do to warm-up. I took it all on board like a kid learning from a teacher and have tried to carry it on through my career. Dan was also a very funny man. He was really dry and all the players enjoyed their time with him. He was a good player, no doubt about it. But like Beni, Bradford probably wasn't the best club for him.

It's easy when you've got good players around you like at Chelsea. But we were inferior to what they were used to. There were no big stars and everyone looked to them to get us out the shit and it wasn't happening.

But Geoffrey couldn't get enough of these famous names. He used to say that Bradford wasn't sexy enough compared with somewhere like Leeds and he thought he could change that by bringing in these top players.

But the results weren't great and we were still struggling. So a few months into the season he tried to pull another rabbit out the hat by signing Stan Collymore. It was the same script as with Beni. All the chairman would tell us was that another great player was on the way

He was already spending massive money on the wages of the ones he'd brought in already. But we were bottom of the table and struggling to score goals. Ashley Ward, our centre forward, had arrived from Blackburn on a lot of money the day before the first game but he still hadn't got off the mark. The manager was under pressure so in came Stan, another Mr Richmond signing.

What can you say about Stan? We'd all read the papers and knew his history. We remembered all the stories about Ulrika Jonsson and getting bombed out of other clubs. We knew about the problems he had with being diagnosed with depression and shit like that. So he was a bit different to most players. How different we quickly found on his first day in training.

Sharpey and I offered to show him how to find the training ground and we jumped in the back of his car. Stan started the engine and this strange hooting noise came out the stereo. What the f*** was that? It only turned out to be a CD of whale music! It was the sort of rubbish you might hear in the background if you're having a massage but Stan just turned it up and drove off. We were sat in the back looking at each other and trying not to laugh.

Then Sharpey had to open his big mouth. "No wonder you were diagnosed for depression, Stan, listening to crap like this." I put my head in my hands. Here we were on his first day at a new club and he's already getting slagged off for being a bit nuts. But Stan was a good lad and a fantastic footballer. If his head had been right, I'm sure he'd have played loads of times for England.

He must have done something right because he was a multi-millionaire playing regularly for Nottingham Forest, Liverpool and Aston Villa in the Premier League. Now he was a big fish in a small pond at Bradford. But he was stranger than anyone I've ever met.

After that first session, we were getting in the showers and Stan got his electric razor out. But instead of doing his chin, all of a sudden he's stood there shaving his bollocks! He's got a leg balanced against the wall, his dick's hanging there for all to see and there are pubes flying all over the floor! The rest of us didn't know where to look.

Was he for real?

Nobody knew what to say – even Dean Saunders was short of a word or two because he was dumbstruck by the sight of this bloke shaving his parts in front of us. When Stan had finished, he put some cream on his bollocks, got dressed, did all his toiletries and walked out the changing room as if nothing had happened.

He was a genuine guy but trouble followed him round and he'd only been with us a couple of weeks when some fella punched him in a nightclub. Stan had done nothing wrong. He was just having a quiet drink with a mate when this Birmingham fan had a go because he used to play for Villa and smacked him on the nose. The papers were soon all over it and there was press everywhere the next day when we went off training.

Stan had a little nick on his nose from a thumb-nail scratch, it was nothing. But the papers were saying that he'd been filled in and had two black eyes and a broken nose. The photographers were outside waiting to get a snap of Stan's so-called injuries. So I thought, let's give them a proper picture. I found this crepe bandage, one of those clingy ones you put on to protect ankles, and pulled it over his head. We could hardly get it on because it was that tight but I cut two holes for his eyes and another around the mouth. He looked like this Egyptian Mummy!

All the press are queuing up outside the door of the changing room and he comes out with this Mummy head on. The cameras didn't stop flashing and it was on every front page the next morning. Nobody knew that all this fuss was about a little scratch on his nose. But that was the baggage he brought with him everywhere he went.

Stan's debut was in the derby with Leeds, live on Sky, and he scored a beauty overhead kick from Beni's cross. It was a brilliant finish but then he ran straight in front of the away fans to celebrate and give them stick and ended up getting into trouble with the FA – but that was typical Stan. He was never out the public eye and a good laugh to have round the changing room. But he was hardly the sort of player you should be bringing in when you're bottom of the table. That was down to Geoffrey, though, not the manager and he just had to lump it.

The team spirit was still pretty high and the players we'd brought in were all good ones but just not the right type at the right time. It was the chairman's money though so nobody else had a look-in.

Geoffrey was such a big influence over Bradford although he would always say that he never picked the team. But I can remember when Stuart McCall was in temporary charge for a couple of games after Chris had been sacked. Stuart went into Geoffrey's office and handed him the team sheet he was thinking of playing that Saturday. They were sat talking for half an hour when Geoffrey passed across a piece of paper with the line-up that he wanted to see out there. From that moment, Stuart decided to stick to playing and not push for the job anymore.

There were rumours that Geoffrey interfered, even when Paul was here, and the Intertoto Cup was probably down to the chairman. But he was usually fine with me. I'd come from Oxford and was very grateful they'd paid nearly a million pounds. And Bradford had given me my first taste of the Premiership.

Geoffrey appreciated that I gave 100 per cent every week and stayed very fit and knew he could rely on me in every game. But he was a sharp businessman as I found out when we were talking about a new contract.

I knew that Stan was on £13,000 a week, Dan £22,000, Beni £42,000, Wardy on £18,000, Wethers £16,000 – all on decent money. My contract was coming up and my agent suggested we went to see Geoffrey about a new deal. I'd scored ten goals the previous season to help keep us up so I felt I was worth the same sort of wages that the others were getting.

We talked about it and Geoffrey sat there smiling and nodding his head. Yes Dean, he said, you've done very well but we're still at the bottom so I'm going to give you three options. Straight away the alarm bells were ringing in my head. What's he going to conjure up here?

But when Geoffrey outlined the ideas, I was pleasantly surprised.

The first option was to double my earnings the following season if we stayed in the Premier League. If we didn't survive, my second choice was to accept an offer for a little bit more but if I didn't want it they could sell me. Or thirdly, he said, they would give me £100,000 at the end of my contract because of the efforts I'd put in for the club.

It wasn't a bad choice and I didn't know what to do. I said I'd have to talk to my agent and come back with a decision later on. Two weeks later Geoffrey sold me to Middlesbrough and I never saw a f****** penny!

EL TEL

THE MOST FAMOUS COACH IN ENGLAND was stood in the tunnel at Valley Parade waiting for me.

We'd just lost 1-0 to Middlesbrough in an FA Cup tie. It was on TV so the crowd was crap and they nicked it with a great goal from Hamilton Ricard. We absolutely battered them but missed loads of chances. Then they scored with an absolute "worldy" in the top corner but that's how it goes when you are struggling like we were.

I thought I'd done all right though – and so did Terry Venables.

As I walked towards our changing room, he stopped me and said so. Dean, you were the best player on the park by a mile. Hearing that from him and shaking his hand, I felt like a million dollars. Even though we'd got beaten again, here was the former England manager telling me how well I'd played. I walked in the dressing room feeling ten foot tall. I tried not to smile because everyone was gutted about the result but talk about a real pick-you-up. It's not every day that one of the best football coaches in the world gives you that sort of pat on the back.

I didn't know at the time but my performance that night was to clinch the next move in my career when I joined Terry at the Riverside. Terry had gone in at Middlesbrough about a month before to help out Bryan Robson. They were struggling as well and while they weren't as deep in the shit as we were, Bryan needed some help.

And you can't ask for a better coach on board than Terry Venables.

I never thought that I would be Terry's first signing but about a week after the cup game they put an offer in. Jim Jefferies didn't want to sell me but it was too good an opportunity for me to turn down. Boro were offering me great money and you don't ignore the chance to work with Terry Venables and Bryan Robson. And hopefully I would be staying in the Premier League – something that wasn't going to happen for Bradford.

We were too far adrift and there was no chance of us staying up. Jim said they wouldn't stand in my way and I didn't need much persuading to go. You don't say no to Terry Venables. I sat there with him, Bryan and the Boro chief executive Keith Lamb as we talked figures.

The deal was fantastic but I would have signed anyway just to play for Terry.

And Middlesbrough are a huge club. You only have to look at the fantastic training facilities, indoor and outdoor. It sure beat the council pitches we practised on at Bradford where you needed a snorkel if it rained because everything was under water.

Working with Terry was all I'd hoped for and more. I'd never had a manager like that before in my life. You would never hear him rant and rave, shout and bawl. He was always on the same wavelength as the players and got his points across so calmly.

As my agent finalised the contract, Terry pulled me into his office to demonstrate the way they would be playing. He wanted me working just off Alen Boksic, the Croatian international centre forward, and drew up this chart to show the areas I should be looking at. He said I didn't need to run around all the time but just stick to these areas and be available for the pass when we had the ball. I walked out the room thinking that I'd learned more in five minutes with him than in five years.

But you could see it was the same with the other lads on the training ground. People like Paul Ince had played for England and Man United and Inter Milan but he still hung on every word that Terry said. There were a lot of big hitters in the squad but they all looked up to him. Every day at training was like an education. I had to pinch myself to realise that this was happening for real.

But I was there because Terry wanted me and I had a job to do. I was reminded of that on my first day when Keith O'Neill, one of the wingers, came straight over and said how good it was to have someone who could put the ball in the back of the net. So the pressure was on.

Terry's man-management skills were second to none. A lot of gaffers only worry about the players who are in the team and if you aren't in the starting 11 you don't exist. But that was never the case with Terry. He would be interested in everybody and I don't just mean the players. He would speak to anyone who worked at the club and knew all their names. You'd see him stop and talk to the masseur, the kit lady, the boot man – he'd always find time for people. And that's what made it so special. Nobody was left out to feel rejected. Terry had this way of making sure everybody mattered in the running of the place which was why the atmosphere around the club was fantastic.

Every training session was different to make sure we went out on a Saturday knowing exactly what our jobs were. Terry would drill it in to you and the message would stick. Once training was finished, he'd be his usual smiling, wise-cracking self and was great company to be around. Though I never got invited down to London to one of his clubs.

It seems a funny situation now that we had Terry and Bryan in charge and I called them both gaffer. But there was never any problem between the two of them. Both would be in the changing room before a game talking to players and passing on advice but there was no confusion. Terry was obviously the boss because Bryan had requested him to come in and help but that didn't mean that nobody listened to Bryan. They worked well as a team together and bounced off each other – you only have to look at our results to see that.

Viv Anderson and Gordon McQueen were still there on the coaching staff although Gordon had just broken his ankle so wasn't very mobile. But Bryan would join in with all the training while Terry tended to concentrate on the team affairs.

I was supposed to make my Middlesbrough debut away to Newcastle in a north-east derby. What a game to start off with at my new club – if only I'd been able to. I was sat there in the hotel where I was staying, eating a pre-match meal with Gareth Southgate. I was really buzzing in my new tracksuit and Boro coat and couldn't wait to get going. I went outside to put my kit bag in the boot of the car. Shit, what's up with my back? As I bent forward to drop the stuff in, I suddenly couldn't move. It was only a few hours to kick off and my back had gone.

I started panicking and just about managed to drive to the training ground where we were due to set off from. I'd rung the physio and explained to him what had happened and as soon as I got there, he had me in his room and was trying to manipulate my back on the table. In walked Terry to ask what was going on and saw his new striker, the first player he had signed for the club, laying flat out in agony. What a start! There was no way I could drive again and Helen had to come up to take me home.

The club gave me a hard mattress to lay on and I was stuck there watching Soccer Saturday while the rest of them were playing in front of 50,000 screaming Geordies. The team news flashed up on Sky and they were talking about Dean Windass missing out because he'd done his back. Then the phone rang and it was my dad laughing and joking that the bag must have contained my wages which was why it was so heavy. But I didn't see the funny side. I was just so annoyed with myself for getting such a stupid injury and gutted to miss such a big game. I could imagine what the Boro supporters were thinking about the new boy. But thankfully we won the game with two goals from Alen which helped to ease the pain a bit.

My back soon healed and I was able to train again and the following week I was in the team at Chelsea – and on the scoresheet with a header. We got beaten 2-1 thanks to a 60-yard backpass from Noel Whelan which gifted them the winner. But scoring on my debut got me back in the good books with the fans and things went well for the rest of that season.

We ended up just below mid-table which was a massive achievement considering that when Terry had come in, we were down there in the bottom three and one of the favourites to get relegated.

But Terry's contract was up after the last game and all the talk was about whether he would decide to stick with us or not.

Having kept us up, there were rumours flying around that Boro would offer Terry a new contract and all the players were desperate for him to stay. Even Incey, who had worked under some great bosses, was trying hard to persuade him because he had learned so much from Terry's time at the club.

I was hoping and praying he'd say yes but the stories would change day by day. We didn't really have a clue what was going on behind the scenes. I don't think Terry himself knew what he wanted at that time. He'd been there to do a job and succeeded and I'm not sure he'd really thought about what to do next.

Players get used to managers coming and going but he was such a nice fella and we didn't want to lose him. And I was his first signing …

But when the news finally came out that Terry had decided to move on it wasn't really a surprise. He'd had a great time but I don't think he wanted to stay long term and now his mission was accomplished it was time for somebody else to step in. What we didn't know at the time was that we'd be swapping one England manager for another …

FINAL CHANCE

I'VE KNOWN STEVE McClaren for a long time – I used to clean his boots at Hull. He was a midfielder at the club when I first came in as an apprentice and I got the job of clearing up behind him.

Steve will tell you he wasn't the best attacking midfield player around. I thought he was a pub player! He was very skinny, like a streak of piss, and looked like he'd get blown over by a gust of wind. Brian Horton used to make him drink Guinness and eat everything to put a bit of weight on.

That was the old-school team at Boothferry Park with Billy Whitehurst, Peter Skipper and Gareth Roberts and he'd have grown up fast. But when I was clearing all the shit off his boots, I never imagined that one day he would be leading out England. It's a fantastic rise from being a Hull City footballer to the national manager but full credit to him. It makes me feel proud. And Steve has never changed. I texted to congratulate him when he got the England job and he sent me a message straight back. Didn't put me in the squad, though!

After Hull, Steve started taking his coaching badges while he was still playing so he was ready to move into the other side of the game. He'd learned his coaching trade at Oxford and Derby and had been the number two to Alex Ferguson at Man United. You couldn't be involved with a bigger club than that.

I'd always have a laugh with Steve whenever Bradford played United. He'd always pull me to one side in the tunnel afterwards and have a joke about the old times. So you can imagine the reaction when we found out he'd got the Boro job. He was laughing his f****** head off.

We were his big chance to make the jump into Premiership management.

There were a lot of changes behind the scenes with all the coaching staff following Bryan out the door. Steve brought in Steve Harrison and Steve Round as well as Bill Beswick, who was a sports psychologist – he was big on that sort of thing.

Steve's methods were very different from Terry and we had a lot of meetings. The first day he took over, he called the players into a big room and there on the wall was one word in big black capital letters: SACRIFICE. We were all muttering and looking at each other. What the f***'s that all about? Steve could see we were a bit suspicious but he sat us all down and told a story about David Beckham.

Steve had once asked Becks what he wanted to do in his football career. I want to be the best player in the world, came the reply. How do you achieve that then, Steve asked. Becks answered that you've got to sacrifice a hell of a lot of things in life. You can't go out with your mates for an extra pint; you can't go sneaking into McDonalds after training; you've got to be dedicated at all times and prepared to sacrifice temptations along the way.

Then Steve pulled out this chart with his five-year plan for the club. And he asked who wanted to be on this journey with him? We were impressed because this was something very new. Steve was concentrating on the mental side of the game as much as the physical one.

Boro were one of the first clubs to bring in Prozone where you track how much ground a player covers during a game. And bringing in Bill Beswick as well encouraged us to think about matches in a different way. Bill never forced his ideas on you; you weren't made to follow his suggestions. But he'd leave letters round the ground from famous sportsmen like Michael Jordan, using positive statements to try and get in your head that way. It was interesting but I'm not sure I can say that the methods definitely worked.

People are different but it did show me how much I had to learn to become a top professional footballer. You learn all the time, which is probably why I've played as long as I have. You pick up things from other players and coaches and see how they live their lifestyles and try out new training methods and techniques.

My relationship with Steve was fantastic, even though I was more out the team than in.

His first game was at home to Arsenal and was a total nightmare. We got absolutely battered 4-0 and they could have scored ten. It was a tough start and he was under a bit of pressure when we lost a few games. I knew he'd pull it round and we soon got some points on the board but I found myself on the bench most matches.

I did feel a bit of a scapegoat at times. I was always the one who got dragged off at home or the one who was left out. If somebody got sent off, it was always me that got sacrificed. It was very frustrating because I'm not the sort of player who does it for the money. That will come along if you are doing the business on the pitch and all I've ever wanted to do is play football.

I still got on fine with Steve and worked very hard in training but he knew I wanted to be playing more and loaned me out to Sheffield Wednesday for a month. I only played a couple of games for them though before I knackered my back and had to come back early.

I got back in the Boro team and played in an FA Cup game against Man United at the Riverside. We beat them 2-0 on a Saturday lunchtime with Noel Whelan and Andy Campbell scoring and that set us off on an unbelievable run.

I was injured for the next round when we beat Blackburn and came back as a sub in the quarter-finals when we did Everton 3-0. All of a sudden we were in the semis against Arsenal at Old Trafford and everybody was desperate to play. But we had a lot of injuries at the time which hit us hard, although it helped me.

The week before the game, we were playing Aston Villa when Whelan did his hamstring after ten minutes. I was on the bench and came on – and knew that suddenly I had a great chance of starting against Arsenal.

Steve broke the news early in the week that I would be playing. I was bouncing off the f****** walls. It was everything that I'd dreamed of since I was a kid, sat in front the telly watching the FA Cup with my dad. Arsenal at Old Trafford in a semi-final – and only 90 minutes away from the final itself.

The build-up to the game was unbelievable. The whole of the town was caught up in cup fever and you couldn't move for people talking about it.

Driving into the stadium was something else. Boro took 30,000 fans that day and every one must have been on the side of the road as we slowly made our way into Old Trafford. It was an amazing sight and I could feel a chill going down my spine.

We ran out for a warm-up and there they all were in the Stretford End – a wall of Boro fans. F****** hell, I'd never heard a noise like it.

Nobody gave us a chance. Arsenal were the holders at the time and we were massive underdogs, especially with the players we were missing. Incey was banned after five bookings, Beni Carbone couldn't play because he was cup-tied and we had a bit of a makeshift side. You looked at the Arsenal teamsheet and they had all the big hitters – Henry, Vieira, Campbell.

But we played them off the park.

In the team talk, Steve told us we had to stop them playing. Don't give Vieira any time, get straight into his face. He was saying this and staring straight at me with this glint in his eye. If you don't stop Vieira, he will win this game single-handed. Steve kept looking across in my direction. It didn't need a rocket scientist to work out what he was thinking.

They kicked off and the ball was played straight back to Vieira. Bang, I hammered him. The ball was bouncing a bit and I launched into him as he tried to bring it under control. Have some of that.

Alen Boksic ran over to me, shaking his head and saying that I shouldn't have done that. But I knew exactly what I'd done – and it was just what Steve had asked for. He didn't want me to go out there and deliberately hurt Vieira but just ruffle his feathers a little bit. Job done and the game wasn't even a minute old.

Vieira needed treatment and had to have strapping on his knee to play the rest of the game. He was very, very quiet and didn't really want to know after that. There's our big chance, I thought. Their main man doesn't like being kicked and that's him out of it. I was so fired up.

After that, it was all Middlesbrough. But the ball wouldn't go in.

We had another injury when Ugo Ehiogu went off with a pulled calf and Gianluca Festa came in. But we still kept battering away at them. Richard Wright pulled off three good saves from me. On a good day I'd have had a hat-trick.

But then they got a corner and scored a fluke goal that went in off Festa. What a way to go 1-0 down in an FA Cup semi-final.

Try as we might, there was no way back and Arsenal somehow hung on. And what should have been the greatest moment in my career turned into the worst one. I was in tears when the final whistle blew. All those years I'd watched an FA Cup final and here I was that close to playing in one and we'd lost. It felt even worse because we had dominated the game. But the only thing that mattered was that Arsenal had got the only goal – a f****** own goal.

Arsene Wenger was very good about it afterwards and told the press that Arsenal had been lucky. The better team had lost. But it was easy for him to say that because they were off to the Millennium Stadium again. We were heading home to drown our sorrows.

It was a very quiet bus as we got to the airport to fly back to Teesside. Bill Beswick said it was the best game he'd ever seen me play but I was too dejected to take it in. At least I've still got Thierry Henry's shirt from that game as a souvenir. It takes pride of place hung up in the hallway at home – I'm not sure if he did the same with mine.

MOVING ON.
AGAIN.

MIDDLESBROUGH NEVER SAW THE BEST OF ME. I wanted to play every week but felt like a bit-part player. Don't get me wrong I know I was good enough for the Premiership and I thought I showed that whenever I did get a game. But I wanted to be involved a lot more.

It was good money and some lads would have been happy to just sit there and collect their wages. But that's not me. I've got to be earning the cash and the only way to do that is to get your boots on and play. But that wasn't happening at Boro.

That's why I ended up going to Sheffield United where I got the best of both worlds. I was on the same money as before but this time I was playing every week.

I didn't get that chance at the Riverside. I'd have loved a run of ten games in the side or even four or five in a row just to get that momentum going. But it didn't happen.

I could see that Steve wanted to use the younger lads. I was 33 and there were other players that he'd pick instead. I understand that and there was no animosity but that didn't stop me feeling frustrated.

I'd played well in the FA Cup semi-final but that didn't change anything. And I knew the writing was on the wall in the summer when Steve brought in an Italian lad Massimo Maccarone from Empoli for a club record £8.15m. You're not going to spend that sort of money and then not play him every week. Maccarone was always going to be the first choice. I was never going to get a look-in.

Massimo couldn't speak any English when he arrived. He took time to settle and blend in with the squad but he was a nice enough lad. On his first away trip there were a group of us playing cards on the bus. It was the usual faces – me, Incey, Ugo Ehiogu, Mark Crossley, Nemeth and Jason Gavin.

We were playing a few hands of three-card brag and Massimo insisted on joining in. We reckoned he'd never played in his life because he got taken for £10,000! The lads felt a bit bad about it and planned to let him off but on the Monday at training, in he walked with all the money and made sure he paid up his debts. Top man.

I think Massimo saw himself as the next Ravanelli at Boro but it never really happened for him. Pity because he was a good lad.

But his arrival meant arrivederci Windass and I was always on the bench or turning out in reserve games. I'd try my hardest even in the shittest surroundings but I couldn't get a look-in. I wasn't looking for a move but I just wanted to be involved somewhere.

The injuries didn't help and I had a problem with my back and then a calf strain. I couldn't get fit and it was really pissing me off. So when I finally did, I went into Steve and asked if I could go out on loan for a month. Somebody, just give me some games. Steve said he'd make some inquiries and Coventry came in. I didn't mind dropping down to the Championship because it was still a decent standard and was only short term to get my fitness up again.

Gary McAllister was keen and that was good to hear. It sounded like a decent move for a few weeks.

The day before I was due to go down there, I was in a jewellers picking up a ring for a mate when the phone rang. It was Stuart

McCall, my old Bradford mate, asking if I wanted to go on loan to Sheffield United. It sounded tempting. Sheffield was only an hour from home, they were higher in the table than Coventry pushing for the play-offs and I knew that Neil Warnock loves his strikers. Macca also said they were a better footballing side.

But there was one slight problem first. I had already told Coventry that I was going there.

I rang my solicitor, John Hendrie, and told him what Stuart had said. Leave it to me, he said, and I'll get it sorted. He did and when I rang Gary back, he was fine about it. He was disappointed but he could understand my position and wasn't going to argue. Stuart had promised me I was going there to play. It wouldn't be another case of sitting on the bench waiting to come on for the last few minutes. Mind you, I knew I had to perform because Warnock had so many forwards he could pick. There was a lot of experience – Paul Peschisolido, Big Chief Wayne Allison, Steve Kabba, Tommy Mooney, Carl Asaba and me.

The gaffer would put three strikers on the bench every week. So if you weren't doing your job, he'd pull you off like a shot. That was his philosophy with the whole team. He was fair with his players and would back them all the way providing they were doing the business. Anyone who let their standards drop would soon know about it. He had no hesitation in leaving you out and didn't give a f*** what you thought. Rob Kozluk found that out after a game at Derby when the lad he was supposed to be marking at a corner scored with a free header. Warnock didn't play him again for two months.

Everyone knew where they stood with him.

But that month at Bramall Lane went like a dream and I got three goals in four games. Everything I touched seemed to go in. Strangely, the first game was at Bradford who were in a right mess at the time. They'd just come out of administration and had no money and they had a team of kids out because of injuries. We hammered them 5-0 and I scored the first. Michael Brown was on fire at the time, scoring for fun, and we'd had a bet of £50 a goal. He never scored that day so that was the first £50 I took off him!

I wore a t-shirt under my shirt that day with the numbers 9.9 on it. That was having a go at Chris Kamara who'd had a pop at me on the telly for being too fat. Steve McClaren had this strict rule that nobody in his squad could have a body fat of more than ten per cent – and I was just under. So the Sheffield United lads thought it would be good for me to show it if I scored.

It was the perfect start to score on my debut and of course I celebrated. I got some stick from the Bradford fans because of it but emotions take over at that moment. It wasn't my fault that I left Bradford – they'd needed the money – but I'd have been a fool not to leave for Middlesbrough.

Bradford got relegated that year but that's football and you've got to move on with your career. The move to Boro was definitely a step up for me at that time. But going to Sheffield United on loan was like a breath of fresh air after all the frustration of not getting games at the Riverside and that month flew by.

The fans were brilliant and were desperate for me to stay. I scored a header in my last game when we won 2-0 at Reading and as I walked to the bus, all these Sheffield United supporters kept stopping me and begging me to sign on for longer. I would have done so there and then but Boro had already made the decision that they wanted me back. So I got my shirt signed by all the Sheffield lads, thinking I wouldn't see them again, and returned to the Riverside, hoping my goal-scoring record might earn me another chance.

Middlesbrough had a few injuries, which is why Steve wanted me back, but nothing much changed and I was on the bench again for the next couple of games.

We were due to play Chelsea at Stamford Bridge in the FA Cup third round. I expected to be a sub again but Steve was impressed with my form and fitness and picked me to play up front on my own with a five-man midfield.

It was a big chance live on TV and I thought I took it. Steve said afterwards I was the best player on the pitch although Chelsea won 1-0. But most people will remember that game for their keeper Carlo Cudicini getting sent off for booting me in the head. Christian Karambeu had put a cross in from the right that was heading straight for Cudicini's hands. I thought I could get it. I looked at the keeper, then the ball. I launched myself at it and ended up smashing Cudicini into the net.

Within seconds it was all kicking off. It was a free-for-all in the net with everybody piling in. There must have been 14 players in that goal all having a go. As I tried to get off the floor, Cudicini brought his knee up towards my face and caught me on the nose. He claimed later that I'd faked it but he definitely kneed me. I got up and went for him but it was pulled apart before it could really get going.

I knew the referee had seen it and when he'd managed to calm everything down he pulled us together. I wasn't going to complain about my yellow card for the challenge but Cudicini couldn't believe it when he got a straight red. I wasn't the most popular person at Stamford Bridge after that and spent the rest of the game listening to 40,000 Cockneys calling me a fat Yorkshire bastard. As if I was bothered ...

We were annoyed about the result but I was really pleased with my performance and I thought that was bound to give me another opportunity in the Premier League. But again it didn't happen.

A week or so later, the gaffer pulled me into his office and said that Warnock had been back on the phone. He wanted me at Sheffield United for the rest of the season and did I fancy it? Absolutely.

All right, it meant the end of my time at Middlesbrough because my contract would be up then. But I was joining a team in the top six of the Championship with a great chance of going up. So if all went to plan, I'd just be putting off the Premiership until next season.

It felt like when I'd joined Bradford four years earlier. I was under pressure to perform from the start.

At Valley Parade, I was the big-money signing. At Bramall Lane, I was the big-time Premiership player. Either way, they expected me to produce the goods. But I love all that. I was the big fish in a small pond and the spotlight from the fans and the rest of the team gave me a real buzz. Warnock piled on the pressure by saying they were paying £5,000 of my wages and he'd never given anyone that kind of money in his life. He had a lot of faith in me and I knew I wouldn't let him down.

Not that I'd see the gaffer much during the week. Kevin Blackwell, his assistant, used to do all the coaching and Neil hardly seemed to be there. People ask if I had a fall-out with him but he was never around me to fall out with. He'd bugger off down to his house in Cornwall for a couple of days and you wouldn't see him until Thursday. You'd train Friday morning, play on the Saturday and then he was off again.

We'd have a double session with Blacky on Tuesday, a day-off Wednesday and then Neil would reappear just in time for the next game at the weekend. But it obviously worked because the results were good and we stayed in the top six the whole time.

We both had strong personalities but Neil was fine with me most of the time. We would clash on occasions but he never got in my way and I never got in his. Whatever went on was down to the fact that neither of us would back down in an argument.

I didn't score that many goals but I still felt I was playing well and contributing to the team. The only thing that pissed me off was the way he would always rotate the strikers. I think the gaffer had too many forwards to choose from so he never knew his best partnership and stuck to it. Instead he'd always be chopping and changing and that got annoying at times. You'd play well for 70 or 75 minutes and then he'd pull you off and throw on the Chief who'd get a tap-in from a yard in the last minute when you'd been working your arse off all game.

But I was starting every week so you put up with it. It was just the way Neil Warnock worked and it obviously did the trick because we made it into the play-offs.

The semi-finals were against Nottingham Forest and we were delighted to draw the away leg 1-1 with Browny getting our goal from a penalty. It was a massive result for us at the City Ground and everyone thought we were virtually through because nobody beat us at Bramall Lane.

We weren't over-confident but with our decent home record, we all fancied finishing the job in front of our own supporters. But before we'd got our heads round it, Forest were 2-0 up and I got dragged off at half-time.

I wasn't happy because I didn't think I had done too badly. Me and Carl Asaba had done quite well and I was surprised to see the board go up. But he brought Kabba on for a bit of pace and then took off Asaba for Pesch. To be fair, the changes worked a treat and we eventually got through 4-3 so I was made up.

We went out into Sheffield afterwards and got steaming drunk. I stayed over in a hotel and was still in the bar at 5am the next day with Michael Brown and Paddy Kenny. It felt brilliant to be in the play-off final and we couldn't wait for Cardiff to come along. What I didn't know was that the substitution had been the final nail in the coffin for me – I was never going to pull on a Sheffield United shirt again.

DARKEST DAY

THE LAGER WAS FLOWING like water. One pint became two, then three, five, eight, ten, maybe even more. But could I get pissed? Could I f***. The more I drank, the more sober I felt. I could still have been there drinking today and it wouldn't have had any effect.

I couldn't get my head round it. This was the biggest game of the season, the biggest of my career and where was I? Sat at the bar of my f****** local.

Sheffield United were playing Wolves in the play-off final at Cardiff and here was Dean Windass 300 miles away, throwing beer down his neck in a pub in Menston.

How had it come to this? Well, there was one good reason for that. Neil Warnock. He was the man responsible for killing my dream of playing in the Millennium Stadium. I never thought I would feel as bad after losing the FA Cup semi-final with Boro. But getting dropped for the play-off final was ten times worse.

I'd been brought in by Neil to do a job and that was to get Sheffield United in the play-offs. Mission accomplished and now we were only 90 minutes away from the Premiership. So what does he do? Tell me to f*** off by bombing me out in the cold.

I wanted to knock his f****** head off. What else was I supposed to think? All that hard work had been pissed against the wall. The rest of the lads were gearing up for a massive final and there was me going out on a bender with some mates. I could have travelled down with the team but what was the point? They wouldn't have wanted me moping around with a sulk on and I'm not one who can pretend that everything's all right when really it's shit.

I had played in the semi-finals against Nottingham Forest. He hadn't said then that I wouldn't be involved any more. Everything had been sorted for Cardiff. I'd got the hotel rooms booked for the family, the tickets were arranged, I'd even had my f****** new suit measured. The kids were really excited. I was really excited.

We'd finished third in the league and were playing really well. Wolves had only just sneaked in and we knew they could be beaten. It was going to be a fantastic day to remember – but Neil Warnock had ruined it for me.

So instead I was propping up the bar in the pub just up the road from home. I wanted to be anywhere but Cardiff.

Of course the telly was on, showing the game. And naturally I wanted to watch it. They were my mates playing out there, only I wasn't with them. It felt strange as the game went on because I was in two minds. I wanted Sheffield United to win for the lads but I didn't for Warnock. As far as I was concerned, he could go and get f*****. So the beer kept flowing. The rounds kept coming and the empty pint glasses stacked up but I still felt nothing inside.

We got turned over 3-0. Wolves were brilliant that day and we never turned up. Would I have made any difference? Who knows, but it would have been nice to have got that chance.

Warnock had dropped the bombshell five days before the game. In the lobby of a five-star hotel in Birmingham of all places. We'd been given a couple of days off after the Forest game before starting to train again. Then he took us to Springs, a posh health club, to get everyone relaxed and away from the pressures of the build-up.

While we were down there, he let us have a few drinks and play some golf at the Belfry. So a group of us got hammered and went off to play a four-ball on the championship course. We all had to drink a shot a hole, it was sambuca or something like that, and we were blitzed. Pesch could hardly drink anyway so he was all over the place.

We got to the 13th tee and I had a massive problem. I was dying for a shit. Of course there were no toilets around but there was no way I could hang on. Drinking these f****** shots wasn't helping – we were hitting about four balls let alone one. I was that desperate to go I disappeared behind the shed at the 13th and ended up having to wipe my arse with a load of leaves. The other lads were pissing themselves and trying to take photos of me on their mobile phones, threatening to send them off to the papers, as I crouched down in the bushes with my trousers round my ankles!

There was a rumour later that I'd shit in the hole. Not true, my aim isn't that good. But I can't imagine Seve Ballesteros or Tiger Woods stepping off the tee on the championship course to go for a number two next to the shed.

That night we were all sat round with Warnock and Kevin Blackwell and I'd had a right skinful. I was being a bit loud and gobby because I'd drunk that much but I wasn't the only one.

Warnock didn't usually drink a lot but he was joining in and we were all having a good chinwag and slagging each other off. It was the usual banter among the lads but I could just sense it then that something wasn't quite right. I don't know how I knew because I'd had that many pints. But it was just from what he was saying and the way he was talking that started the alarm bells ringing. He was saying how Kabba had done well and what a difference Pesch made when he came on; little things like that which made me wonder if I was going to be left out.

The following morning, the Wednesday before the final, we were due to drive back to Sheffield. I was travelling with Paddy Kenny and just as we were leaving the hotel, Neil Warnock pulled Paddy over. He shouted him over about his contract so I took Paddy's keys and said I'll bring the car round. But Warnock wanted to see me as well. I sat in the other room while Paddy had his chat and then Neil came in.

"This is the hardest decision I've ever made in my managerial career," he said. "But I'm not going to play you in the final. "We need a little bit of pace with Stevie Kabba and I also thought Asaba did well in the semi-final. Sorry Dean, there's no place for you …"

I just lost it.

"Are you f****** winding me up? You've brought me here to get to the play-off final which we have done and now you're dropping me!" All right, the semi-final might not have been my best game but I felt I'd contributed all the way through. And being one of the more experienced players, I knew I could handle the atmosphere and tension at Cardiff.

I called him a c*** and he agreed with me. I was devastated. And if that wasn't a big enough blow to the system he then turned round and said that I wasn't going to be on the bench either because he wanted to have a spare goalkeeper in the five substitutes. He never ever did that but was worried about having no cover if Paddy got injured. I think Antti Niemi had pulled his thigh for Southampton while taking a goal kick in the FA Cup final and he couldn't afford to risk something like that happening without anyone to come in. So he was going to put Alan Kelly on the bench which meant there was no room for me. He was f****** taking the piss now.

Bearing in mind that I'd bought over 30 tickets for the final and paid for three hotel rooms where we were staying. But he still wanted me to travel with the squad! I couldn't do that. I was absolutely gutted and I didn't want that rubbing off on the lads. But what really got to me was when Warnock asked me to say that I'd got a groin strain and was out injured. There was no way I was doing that. He'd made the big decision so it was down to him to respond to it.

If we hadn't been sat in that hotel, I'd have knocked him out there and then. I was that pissed off. Warnock said he'd understand if I did hit him. But it wouldn't have achieved anything.

I told him I wouldn't be coming to the final and he offered to buy all the tickets off me and get my money back from the hotel. He was trying to make it up to me but it was no consolation – not even close. I stood up, shook his hand and walked straight out the door. And that was the last time I saw him as a Sheffield United player. There was the offer of another year written in my contract but I had to tell them by August 1 if I wanted to stay. No way after what had happened.

The rest of that week was a daze and the day of the play-off final was an experience I would never want to repeat. It felt so weird. I was like the best man preparing to do his speech, putting away pint after pint and not feeling any worse for it. People were staring at me and I knew what they were thinking. What the hell is he doing in here with a lager in his hand when he should be on that TV screen right now?

Neil left Stuart McCall out as well and played Mark Rankine in midfield. That was another big call and it all went tits up for him.

I was gutted for the lads because they were a great bunch but maybe he had picked the wrong team. Hindsight's a wonderful thing and playing me and Stuart may not have made any difference. But the result couldn't have gone any worse.

Warnock told the press that I'd walked out on the club which did hurt me. The Sheffield United fans were fuming but that wasn't true at all. I went on a sports phone-in on the local radio and explained my situation. He'd made me out to be the bad boy but it was never like that.

I told John Hendrie that I could never play for that man again. And a few days later Bradford City were on the phone. But fair play to Neil, he didn't bear a grudge and I got a call on my mobile on the morning of my first match back for Bradford.

It was a private number and when I answered it, there was Neil wishing me all the best. I wasn't too surprised but I was flattered and it showed that there was no animosity whatsoever. What had happened was in the past; it was water under the bridge. The manager had made a decision and he'd stuck to it. Whether it was right or not didn't matter anymore.

I want to be a manager one day and who knows, I could be put in the same position. Would I handle it any differently? I won't know until it happens. At the time I was devastated but afterwards I respected him for his decision. And full credit to him for giving me the courtesy call later because he didn't need to do that.

But when it comes to dealing with players, Neil doesn't give a f*** about anyone else apart from himself. Everyone else will tell you that – he'll even tell you the same. He's not bothered if people get hurt because that's always been the way it works and when you look at his record as a manager it's hard to argue.

THE MANAGER'S VIEW

BY NEIL WARNOCK

THERE'VE ONLY BEEN A FEW occasions throughout my career when I've really felt sorry for a player when leaving them out, and Dean was one of them.

He'd done well for us and he's a very good professional, irrespective of what the public view is of him. It was just one of those things – I had to pick my best side and that's what I did. I felt we needed more pace.

Also, I've only used a substitute keeper a few times and they've all been for major games when there was no way around it. If the keeper had got injured after five minutes I could put Phil Jagielka in goal, but who'd replace him?

I knew the easy thing to do would be to leave Dean in because I knew I'd get some stick off him. But I had to go with what, in my mind, was my best team. If he hadn't been annoyed at being left out of such an important game, there'd have been something wrong with him. But, oh God, he said a few words!

What's good about that though, is I've been in exactly the same situation. I was left out of a big cup game for Rotherham against

Leeds United. I'd been picked and the match was then fogged off. We had a game in between and a week later I was left out of the biggest game of my career. I couldn't believe it. Jackie Charlton and all the rest were in that Leeds team.

So I knew how emotional Dean was going to be. When you're not playing and you think you should be playing, no matter what anyone says, you can't just take that on the chin. I certainly don't think you can.

A couple of times when I left players out, they slaughtered me. But that didn't bother me because usually I wanted them to leave the club anyway. With Dean it was different because he'd scored a few goals and he'd done well.

That day I also left Stuart McCall out. With hindsight, we needed Stuart's calming influence, but we can all get it right after the event. Managers live and die by their decisions.

I've spoken to Dean on a number of occasions since then. I've phoned him when I thought he deserved a pat on the back because he did ever so well scoring goals for Bradford.

I know he wants to be a manager and I think he'll do a decent job because he's seen it all. He'll be able to deal with people like himself! Dean talks a lot of sense as well when you get him one-on-one. He's always talking as if he's the captain when he's on the pitch and he'll want to get his own ideas across.

Things like the incident with me will only stand him in good stead because sure as hell, it will happen to him at some stage.

After facing relegation with Oxford I was now promoted with Bradford. Brilliant! I could look forward to facing the likes of Manchester United, Liverpool and Arsenal every week. (L-R... Gareth Whalley, Peter Beagrie, Lee Mills, Me, Lee Sharpe).

Mixing it with the top lads. I'm having words with Chelsea's John Terry while Marcel Desailly looks on.

Pulling the trigger against Sunderland.

Here's me while at Middlesbrough trying to get past West Ham's Stuart 'Psycho' Pearce.

Me and Robbie Savage doing the tango.

Celebrating a goal for Sheffield United against Crystal Palace in 2002. I'd get booked for that now.

Me and Josh in November 2005. He was playing for Huddersfield Town under 12s at the time and I was at Bradford. We were playing Huddersfield that weekend - hence the pose.

Another new hair-do. I'm the Yorkshire Dave Beckham. Honest.

I've just scored a header against MK Dons at the start of the 2005/2006 season. I'm legging it to the touchline to celebrate. I felt a bit daft when it was ruled out for offside.

Back in my hometown colours. Here I'm trying to get past Andy Hughes of Norwich City.

Opposite page: Me and Helen with Josh and Jordan.
We renewed our vows in March 2007 at Menston Methodist Church.

Not too bad for a fat lad.

Just the 104-year wait ...

Worried?
Me?
Course
not!

Lining up to meet the official guests.

Getting stuck into a tackle. Just like any other game.

Yes, I've just scored the best goal ever seen at the new Wembley.

Do you love me or what?

You lovely sod. Giving the hallowed turf a smacker.

Just give us a minute before I speak.

Lovely bubbly, it's champagne time!

Hands up, if
you're going up.

Sorry gaffer,
I never got to
20 goals this
season.

We're all going on a Premier League tour.

I always love a hat-trick.

It's going to be a Hull of a party.

Health and safety? Pah.

Well Ash, told you we'd get there in the end.

BACK ON PARADE

ADMINISTRATION. I didn't even know what it meant. But I soon found out after going back to Bradford. Within a year, I felt like a f****** accountant. We all did.

I knew the shit had hit the fan the year before when the money ran out. All that time paying massive wages for people like Beni Carbone had caught up with them. Bradford went into administration and had nearly gone under.

So why did I go back? I knew that staying with Sheffield United was out the question so I asked John Hendrie to look around for another club. Paul Jewell wanted to sign me again for Wigan but the money was better from Bradford. And to be honest, I didn't want to travel anymore. The kids were settled at school and Wigan was an hour and a half away every day. Bradford's training ground was 15 minutes.

Richmond had gone the year before and the chairman was now Gordon Gibb working alongside Julian Rhodes, who'd been there since the start. Gordon asked me if I wanted to sign a two-year deal and he assured me the finances were fine. Bradford had been in trouble but he said that everything was on an even keel once again. Having been in administration once before, nobody thought it could happen again. I should have known it was too good to be true.

I liked Nicky Law, the manager. He told it to you straight and there was no bull-shitting. I had played against him before when he was a defender at Rotherham. He had curly hair in those days not like the bald-headed bastard who was now my manager. But we got on brilliantly. I knew his football pedigree and he was another strong character. You had to be to deal with all the shit that came our way.

They always say never go back and it was totally different to the first time. The squad was paper-thin.

In the early days you'd look round the dressing room and see good players everywhere, decent lads like Dean Saunders, Peter Beagrie, Stuart McCall, Gareth Whalley and Jamie Lawrence. Lads who were good on the ball but also knew how to mix it – lads who suited playing at this level. If we'd had that team again in that league we'd have done all right. Even four years on. But Nicky had to scrape by with a mix and match squad.

There were a few senior pros like me, David Wetherall and Peter Atherton but also a lot of young lads who'd not experienced it before. So I knew it was going to be hard. Nicky had asked me where I wanted to play. He rang while I was on holiday in La Manga and was asking what shirt number I'd like and things like that. He was going to play me behind just behind the front two but I ended up playing everywhere.

I struggled that year as much as the team. I never get injured but I missed a chunk of the season after a double hernia operation and probably tried to come back too soon. I only got six goals but ironically that still made me the team's top-scorer which says it all.

We'd started off the season quite well and came back from 2-0 down to get a draw with Norwich on the opening day. We also won at Crystal Palace which was something Bradford had never done in their history.

But Nicky was pissing against the wind. He had no chance. He tried to keep everyone concentrating on the football side but it was difficult because he couldn't bring in the players he'd have wanted to.

Gordon and Julian had pushed the boat out to get me there on a two-year contract and they couldn't do any more for him. We just had to get on with it.

I got my first goal against Sheffield United of all teams. And then got sent off. Nicky was massively under pressure and I was fired up for the game. It was live on Sky and I wanted to put on a show against Warnock's team. Wetherall was injured so Nicky put me captain. It was a big honour and I told him he wouldn't regret it.

The game had only been going ten minutes when a throw-in was flicked on and I half volleyed it past Paul Gerrard, my old Oxford team-mate. It flew in the bottom corner. That was my first goal back for Bradford and what a time to get it. Maybe our luck was changing?

Was it f***! They came back to win 2-1 and the worst thing was that Stuart McCall got the winner.

That was his first goal for them but Stuart refused to celebrate. He didn't want to upset our fans who have always worshipped him. I think he was a bit embarrassed as well because he'd shinned it. It came out to him on the edge of the box and must have bobbled about 12 times on the way in. Stuart was Bradford through and through and didn't want to see us get relegated so it must have been strange for him.

It was a kick in the teeth for us and I just lost it at the end. I was chasing a ball with Michael Brown into the corner and launched him. Michael knew I was going to do it and I kicked him up the arse. I'd let myself down and apologised afterwards but that was another f****** fine I had to pay.

Nicky kept battling on but we were still struggling. He went 3-4-1-2 at Crewe with me playing behind the strikers and we got a good point with an overhead kick from Paul Evans, one of our midfielders. It was a real worldy, as good a goal as you'll see. Then Nottingham Forest came to ours and nicked it in the last minute through Andy Reid. We'd played well and got nothing for it again.

We went to Coventry on bonfire night and absolutely battered them. It was the best we'd played all season but we couldn't score. I should have buried a header at the end but it went over the bar and the game finished 0-0. Nicky got the sack three days later.

Julian and Gordon called a meeting with me, Wethers, Athers and Wayne Jacobs and told the four of us we were in charge until they made a new appointment. Peter Atherton had been out injured for six months, Wayne Jacobs had a groin strain, Wetherall was out with his abductor and I was playing and captain. I was also the only one who had the UEFA B licence coaching qualification.

We were due to play at Stoke on the Saturday and we had to decide who was going to take over. Wethers didn't want to do the touchline job so he was going to sit upstairs; Athers was ready to start playing again; I was in the team and captain so I suggested we gave the job to Wayne. He was intelligent and sensible and we knew he was keen to get into the coaching side. He was the obvious choice to take the team.

I've known Wayne Jacobs all my life, played with him and we're very good friends. I'd never had any disagreements with him whatsoever. But when we came to doing a bit of team play in training on the Thursday, I thought he'd lost it. He had me playing left of a three up front in a practice game. I'd been playing down the middle or behind the front two. Being put out on the left wasn't my position. I didn't want to play there. I couldn't play there because I've never had the pace to do that role.

He wanted to know what my problem was so I told him. We'd done well the week before away to Coventry so why the sudden change of formation. My philosophy has always been that if it aint broke then why fix it? But maybe the power he'd been given had gone to Wayne's head a little bit. He took charge and wanted to stamp his own authority on things but taken it a bit far.

I was top goalscorer so why wasn't I playing in my normal

position? What was the point of giving me a role that I knew I couldn't do? I lobbed my bib on the floor and watched the rest of the session sat in the dug-out. I didn't see the point of carrying on.

The following morning I was getting changed when the kitman Barry Wood said Wayne wanted me in his office. I just started laughing. His office! It has gone to his head now.

Wayne was sat behind the desk and told me to shut the door. Then he told me I wouldn't be playing tomorrow. You're having a laugh, I said. But he wasn't smiling. He had decided I wasn't in the right frame of mind and I'd be a sub instead. F*** off, I'm not being sub. If I can't get in this team I might as well pack in now.

We were down the bottom, I was the top goalscorer, and Wayne was leaving me out just to score a few brownie points. He told me to have the weekend off but I still went to the game. I had the right to go and I sat in the stand behind the goal with the fans. And they had one shot on target all game, a free-kick from Nicky Summerbee, and got beat 1-0.

Colin Todd was also in the crowd getting ready to take over with Bryan Robson. Colin was going to be the assistant.

Bryan got the job on the Monday morning and Wayne came in the changing rooms like any other player. He walked straight over to me and shook my hand. There was no animosity. He had a decision to make like Neil Warnock. I think he'd got it wrong but there was no bitterness about it. The Stoke game had gone and we just moved on. Wayne is a genuine man and I've always got on with him. Sometimes you don't see eye to eye in football but you don't hold a grudge and let it affect you. I got on with it; he got on with it and we went out for our first session with Bryan.

The team who'd played on the Saturday were doing a cool down while the rest of us were just running. And Bryan's first words to me were: "I can't believe you can't get in this f****** team."

It was amazing to think that Bryan Robson was manager of

Bradford City. No disrespect but nobody would have thought he'd be interested in a job at Valley Parade. But he was keen to get back into football after being out since leaving Middlesbrough and the chairman saw it as the chance to raise the profile of the club and bring the fans back. And it worked – for the first game at least.

We came back from two down at half-time to beat Millwall 3-2 and everyone thought this was the start of something special. It was a dream start for Bryan - then we lost five on the bounce!

Bryan had the same problems as Nicky. He brought in Ronnie Wallwork from West Brom and a couple of other lads on loan but the money still wasn't there. And then everything went belly-up when the relationship broke down between Gordon and Julian. We thought that financially it was okay and then all of a sudden, the club were back in dire straits.

Pretty soon nobody knew what was going to happen from one day to the next. The club were in administration for a second time and we were all in the dark.

We had meetings with the administrators all the time. We'd sit there and they'd talk this bollocks about deferrals and things like that and you wouldn't have a clue what they meant.

I didn't understand what was going on; I'm not that clever to understand all the financial jargon. All I wondered was whether the club was going to crack up and end up folding. We weren't even sure whether we'd get paid at the end of the week and they couldn't pay us the full amount anyway. At one stage I was deferring 80 per cent of my wages.

It was a very difficult time because, however much you tried to just focus on the football, it was always there at the back of your mind. Am I going to get paid? Don't get me wrong, I was one of the fortunate ones. People like myself and Wethers had earned a little bit through our career already so we had money to fall back on. But the younger lads didn't and that's who I felt sorry for. It must have been really tough for the kids who didn't have any cash behind them and still had mortgages to worry about.

Footballers are working class people. It doesn't matter if you're on £1,000 a week or £100,000 a week. At the end of the day, if you don't get your wages you aren't going to be able to pay the bills. Everybody has to earn a living and put food on the table for their family. But what was going to happen to some of the younger lads if suddenly there was no football club? Nobody was guaranteed a move somewhere when you've got something like 1,000 footballers out of work every summer and the game was all that most of these kids had ever known. They couldn't just walk into another job.

I'd never been relegated before. This was the first time and it felt horrible. But with all the shit flying about off the field, football results had seemed the least of our problems. The players and the supporters were more worried about whether they'd still have a club for next season.

IN THE RED

THE CLUB was telling us to get fixed up elsewhere because everyone genuinely thought that was it. The situation looked that bad.

I was in the office when Paul Heckingbottom, who'd been named our player of the year the previous season, was the first to go. He signed for Sheffield Wednesday and we were all being encouraged to look around.

Darlington were keen to get me and offered a two-year contract. David Hodgson was the manager but I knew his assistant Martin Gray very well because we'd played together at Oxford.

In an ideal world, I wouldn't have thought about it but with everything going pear-shaped at Bradford I had to do something. This was a fall-back because I still wanted to keep playing – at least I'd have the chance if it went tits up at Valley Parade.

I was walking round Morrison's with the missus when the phone rang. It was Colin Todd asking me if I'd decided what to do.

Colin had taken charge when Bryan Robson left the club a month after the season had ended. You couldn't really blame Bryan for going after all the broken promises about the club's finances. He'd got back into football management again but he didn't want all this shit to drag him down. Bryan's contract had run out and he was looking for something bigger than Bradford – and a bit safer. So Colin was the gaffer now. He was probably the only one who would have taken the job in our position. At least he knew about the skeletons in the cupboard and he was surprisingly upbeat given everything that was going on.

I told him about Darlington and how they really wanted me up there. But Colin told me to hang fire and bear with it for a couple more days. Pre-season was just around the corner and I was getting worried but the gaffer said there was still hope.

We were due back for training on July 1. That was the same day they were making a decision on whether to close the gates at the club. I drove into the ground and there was a TV crew from Calendar, the local station, outside the car park. They wanted to know what was going on. F****** hell, so did we!

The players were all in the dark and we weren't sure whether to come in for training or stay away. There was always the danger that you'd get injured and would you be insured if the club no longer existed? My mind was spinning as I walked into the dressing room, not knowing what might happen from one minute to the next.

It was great to see all the lads again – it always is after the summer break – but you could feel the tension in the air. It was a horrible sensation. The gaffer was in a meeting with Julian Rhodes and some of the other coaching staff.

I'd had enough of this and just burst in, demanding to know where we stood. Colin had a smile on his face. Julian had come in at the last minute and baled the club out – Bradford City were still alive.

Colin got straight on the phone and rang David Hodgson to tell him there would be no deal. I was going nowhere. That suited me fine because I wanted to stay anyway. I was desperate for the club to get sorted out and now it had been. We knew that money would be tight as ever but at least Bradford was still going.

Training that morning was great because of the huge sense of relief. We could concentrate on football again and getting fit without wondering whether the next day would be your last at the club. Now we could look ahead and focus on the job of trying to get straight back up again.

It was the first time I'd been relegated as a player and that took a lot to get over. Having played so long, it was a record I was proud of and now that had been shattered which was a big blow to me. But there are two ways you deal with that sort of disappointment. You either shrug your shoulders and give up or get your head down and work extra hard to put it right as quickly as possibly.

That pre-season I ran my tits off. It was the best I can ever remember. I felt great and I was playing well in the friendlies and scoring loads. I got five goals in one game against Farsley Celtic and I just thought everything was coming together at the right time. The previous season had been very hard for me but my confidence was back up again and I couldn't wait to kick off.

The bookies had us down as relegation favourites because of all the problems we'd had off the field. You can't blame them but I knew we were much better than that. I hadn't played at that level of football for ten years since leaving Hull for Aberdeen and I knew I'd be a marked man. Not being big-headed but people would see me as a big fish in a small pond.

At 35, I was also coming to that stage of my career when I'd be up against young lads who were probably still at school when I was playing in the Premier League. They want to mark all the big-hitters and in League One circles, that meant me.

The team spirit was fantastic after everything that had gone on. All the crap had brought everyone closer together and we were out to show the world that Bradford City were still alive and kicking. The gaffer didn't have any money to play with but he managed to bring in a few new faces. Steve Schumacher, who had been captain of England under-18s, came in from Everton along with another young lad Michael Symes and we got Lee Crooks, who'd been around a bit, in from Barnsley. We were just glad to see 20 people on the training ground again. I think we only had six or seven at the start of pre-season.

Colin did a brilliant job to get all these players for next to nothing. Paul Henderson, our Aussie goalkeeper, was picked up walking along Manningham Lane with his rucksack! At least it seemed like that. He came in asking for a trial in a friendly against Bolton and looked like Peter Schmeichel. He was a revelation for us.

The fixture list was an eye-opener. When you're used to playing the likes of Sunderland, Wolves and Birmingham then to see names like Hartlepool, Torquay and Peterborough was a shock to the system. It was a bit of a comedown but there was no point moping and we just got on with it.

We lost the first game to Hartlepool but then went on a great run early on. I was on fire and was convinced we could go straight back up. Colin was brilliant because he only wanted me to play the width of the penalty box. He didn't want me running down the channels or wasting my energy anywhere else. He told me to stay in the danger area and score goals, which I was doing.

Tim, from the local radio station, had £100 on me at 18-1 to finish top goalscorer in the division. After every game, I'd ring him to find out if my main rivals Pawel Abbott at Huddersfield or Hull's Stuart Elliott had got any more goals.

I was helped massively by Nicky Summerbee, who was brilliant on the right wing. I scored 27 goals that season and Buzzer must have set up 18 or 19. Kevin Phillips once scored 30 goals in the Premier League when Nicky was at Sunderland and he was putting them on a plate for me. I was gutted to see him go later that season.

Buzzer would go mad if you didn't get the ball out to him all the time. He could be a right moaning bastard! But give him the ball and you could pick the exact spot where he'd deliver the cross. He wasn't slow but he wasn't one of those wingers who just tries to burn the full back for pace each time and get to the byline. Buzzer would look for that half a yard and then over it would come. He was the best crosser of a ball I've ever known. Nicky had been a great player over the years and Colin knew his strengths. I certainly got the benefit from that.

But if only we'd had someone else to chip in with goals. Managers always say you need a 20-goal a season man and then another one who'd get you 15 and sadly we didn't have that. That's what cost us. If we'd had another striker weighing in with a few goals to help me then I know we'd have got promotion that year. But we just fell short.

We'd had the club's best run for years earlier that season when we won five on the bounce in October. It took us up to second and we were away to the leaders Luton. It was a massive game, the biggest Bradford had been involved in since the Premier League, and loads of fans made the trip down there. They were a very good side with Steve Howard, the big centre forward, scoring for fun but a win that day would have lifted us just one point behind.

The lads were flying because the run we were on and everybody fancied it. We knew they were going to be aggressive and very physical but we were ready for it. Or so we thought. Unfortunately we never turned up. We got battered 4-0 and didn't get a kick all afternoon.

Referee Joe Ross didn't give us anything. Not that we deserved much but every little decision went Luton's way. He was on my case every time I went down on the floor. F****** hell, you're shit, just get up. But once you had a little bit of banter back, he wouldn't have any of it.

We'd let ourselves down big time on the day but the referee didn't help us. And I'd had enough of it. He started taunting us by going "4-0, 4-0" with his fingers and saying we should "sort our defence out". Was I hearing it right? Was the referee taking the piss?

At the end of the game I collared him and told him he'd been a disgrace. And I knew exactly what was coming next. As soon as I started to have a go back, out came the red card. We were walking off the pitch at the time but he couldn't get that card out quick enough. He was so arrogant and horrible and all the players saw what was going on. But we had no comeback because the linesman was always going to back him up all the way.

The gaffer was furious when he heard I'd been sent off after the final whistle and stormed into the referee's room to have a pop so he was in trouble as well. It was no surprise that we both got charged by the FA with bringing the game into disrepute and were sent to a hearing at Birmingham City's ground. Neither of us thought we'd done anything wrong but we were being treated like criminals and walking into that room felt like being in court.

There was a panel from the FA sat at one end of the table like judges and Colin, his assistant Bobby Davison and I were at the other. Mr Ross was further along the table getting quizzed while the linesman was speaking for him on the phone.

Colin was kicking me under the table every two minutes while he stared at Mr Ross. His eyes never left him. I was nearly pissing myself laughing – I thought Colin was going to snap at some point and go over and chin him.

Colin had been accused of calling Ross a c***, which he'd denied. Mr Ross was shaking his head and obviously I didn't know who was telling the truth because I hadn't heard the conversation that had gone on in the referee's room. Colin insisted he'd never used that word. He'd called him a twat.

I was trying not to crack up.

The bloke quizzing him then flicked over a page of his file. "So, Mr Todd, in 1994 when you were the Bolton manager did you not go into the room of another referee and call him a c*** as well?"

"Yes, that's right," Colin replied, "But I've grown up a lot since then."

I just buried my head; I was laughing that much. Not that the FA panel were too amused by all this. It was that funny I daren't look at Colin. But then it was my turn.

"Mr Windass, have you ever been in front of the committee before?"

I hadn't so I told him. Then he started flicking his book over once again.

"Well in 1995, when you were playing for Aberdeen, is it true you got the equivalent of three red cards and got banned for six weeks?"

"Yes, that's right," I said, "But that was in Scotland which is a lot different to here."

I don't think he was too impressed.

"Well, Mr Windass, you haven't had a very good reputation have you?" All the time Colin was staring at me and I could feel his eyes burning into me while he was still giving me a dig under the table.

I knew they wouldn't believe me and they didn't. Mr Ross had sat there and they'd believed every word he had said. Colin and I were sent outside and told to wait like a couple of naughty schoolboys outside the headmaster's office as they discussed the verdict.

I got done £750 and Colin got £500 but I don't think he ever paid it. Mr Ross got away with it and was refereeing again two weeks later. But look at him now. He's running the line. I like to think the FA have seen the light where Mr Ross is concerned.

But the standard of refereeing nowadays is something that pisses everyone off. You only have to look at the Premier League where the refs are all full-time and they do think they are bigger than the players. Graham Poll and Phil Dowd and people like that are earning £60,000 a year and think they are the business.

Let's be fair, some of them are good. All players want is to have a bit of banter. It's an emotional game and you say things in the heat of the moment. I'll have a go at referees but then you'll get some who come straight back and tell you to shut up and get on with it. And I respect them for that.

There's nothing wrong with having a bit of craic as long as you know where to draw the line. You just want people to show some commonsense at times.

Some referees know the way you play and they are well aware if you are trying to con them into winning this decision or that. Others will referee you by reputation. That was the problem in Aberdeen. I was getting pulled up for everything.

If you show six studs up in a tackle then you will get the yellow card. That's always been the case in Scotland and everyone knows that. But I was getting penalised in every challenge. It was getting to the ridiculous stage where I couldn't tackle anybody or make any physical contact.

I'd go up for headers and put in a tackle and the referee would blow every time. I was getting booked week after week for nowt. You do get away with things a bit more in England. You try to be clever by backing into centre halves and making it difficult for players but that's part of the game.

Some referees have never kicked a football in their life and I don't think they really know the game. They might know the rulebook back to front but do they understand what really goes on? That's why I'm all in favour of professional footballers wanting to referee. I'd love to do it myself. But like anyone, we'd have to start off at grassroots level and referee Sunday League games. And there's no way you would get ex-players doing that because they will get dog's abuse. You'd be fighting every Sunday morning.

Big Tony Philliskirk, who used to play for Bolton, went into it but he had to pack in because everyone was waiting to have a pop at him.

All right, nobody's got the divine right to referee a Premier League game but he could have started with the reserves and got some experience that way. But to go down to Sunday League is a load of bollocks. No wonder footballers don't want to do it. But just imagine the difference if you did get an ex-footballer refereeing our game. He'd know the score with things like using your elbows for leverage when you go up for headers. That's one that a lot of referees have you for but how are you expected to jump otherwise without using your arms? Try it and see what I mean.

I've had some good times with referees when I've got a way with a lot but there are plenty more who don't let anything go. They can't wait to blow that whistle.

I got another red card two months after the Luton game. We were playing Wrexham at home on Boxing Day and I'd known the referee Carl Boyeson for years. He used to referee me when I was a Sunday league player in Hull and he'd always run the line in the reserve games at Boothferry Park.

On Christmas Day, Boyo and his dad had been drinking with my old man in their local pub. I think Boyo was only on the orange but they'd had a bit of a laugh about refereeing me the next day. I was talking to Boyo about it before the game and thought I'd be able to get away with a few things after that. But the bastard sent me off after half an hour. I went up for a header in midfield and he blew for a foul. I lost it and we had a bit of an argument.

To be fair, I went over to him with an aggressive manner shouting and swearing and he showed me a straight red for foul and abusive language. I couldn't believe it. I was out of order and probably gave him no choice. But the last thing I expected was to be sent for an early bath by the bloke who'd bought my dad a pint to celebrate Christmas 24 hours before.

I was steaming and waited for him in the tunnel after the game. I'll see you in Hull, I warned him, then we'll sort this out. But Boyo just ignored me and carried on walking past. Just as well really, otherwise I'd have got myself in a load more trouble. I'd stepped over that line again and I didn't get away with it. But I did get revenge of a kind a while later at a charity match.

A friend of the family Terry Allinson had died and we organised a charity game for him. I was happy to play because Terry had been a great bloke and was really close to my dad. He'd also take my wife and Debbie training and knew everyone really well. We arranged this game for a Sunday morning and Boyo was refereeing. We'd sorted everything out about Wrexham by then and had a chat on the phone but this was the first time we'd been on the same pitch since.

I was on the ex-Tigers team with all the old Hull players and with about ten minutes left, I asked Boyo if he fancied swapping jobs. So he went on our team and I took over as the referee.

Boyo was going round trying to kick people but he was that fat he couldn't get near anybody. Finally he ended up booting this lad so I gave the free-kick. Boyo played up to the crowd and came over to give me a mouthful. Straight away there was only one outcome. Foul and abusive language? Off you go, son.

I stuck the red card in his face and gave him his marching orders. So we're even now at 1-1, Boyo! He's actually quite a good friend and, looking back now, he did right to send me off that day. I had lost it and he had a job to do.

Boyo reffed us again the last game of that season when Bradford went to Oldham. I was going for top goalscorer and he gave the most dubious penalty our way for a foul on Wethers that never was. I think he was trying to get back in my good books!

PREMIERSHIP CALLING

THAT FIRST YEAR BACK in League One was a great time for me. To finish as the division's top scorer along with Stuart Elliott on 27 was a real achievement to look back on. I also got named the division's player of the month for August, something that hadn't happened to me since I'd been at Hull, so everything went well personally. The only downside was that we never got into the play-offs.

We won some great away games but the home form let us down. We had a lot of inexperienced lads in the side and I think the pressure got to them a little bit. Away from Valley Parade it was fine because there wasn't the weight of expectation from the supporters. But at home, you were expected to win every week and when that didn't happen you could see some of the younger ones starting to crumble.

The fans were getting on their case but you can't blame them because we had started the season so well. We'd raised the bar and it was down to us to keep that going. Colin kept telling the supporters not to get carried away. By his reckoning we were lucky to still be in this league, never mind pushing for promotion. But it was inevitable after the first couple of months that everyone was going to get excited. I was just the same as any of the fans.

I thought we had enough in the changing room to get promoted and I was as disappointed as those in the stands that we tailed off towards the end. I equalled Elliott from a free-kick which I bent over the wall and into the bottom corner. I spent the rest of the game looking up at Tim in the press box and making sure that Hull hadn't scored any more.

Colin was delighted for me but straight away threw down the challenge to do it again. The season had only just finished and he was already looking ahead and asking me how many goals I'd get next time. I always set myself a target each season but I'll never tell the press or it can make you look stupid. But I mentioned to Colin that I was looking at 15 at least – and I ended up with 20. I might have been another year older but I knew I could still get goals. What I didn't know was that my form was going to earn me the chance of another crack at the Premiership.

For the second year in a row we kicked off at Hartlepool. This time we played them off the park, winning 2-0 and I got one of the goals. As a striker, getting off the mark on the first day of the season is a massive confidence boost. However many years you've been playing, you are always looking for that opening goal to get off and running.

I'd gone on a golf holiday in the summer to La Manga for an ex-players charity do. Alan Ball, the England legend, came over and we got talking about how many goals I'd scored the previous season.

"You've done brilliantly Deano," he said, "but you start again on zero now." And he was spot on. You could enjoy the moment and the glory of finishing top of the pile but the new season meant a new challenge. Every year you have to go out there and prove yourself.

My success did come at a cost and I found people were marking me a lot closer than before. Suddenly you'd have centre-halves following you all over the place. If I went for a piss there would probably be someone in there with me. It was flattering in a way though it did mean I got kicked a lot and picked up more bumps and bruises.

We drew Rochdale in the first round of the Carling Cup. It hardly sounded the biggest game of the season but it had a massive impact for me.

Bradford had struggled big time in the cups over the years and I think it was four years since they had won one. We were desperate for a cup run – FA Cup, League Cup, Auto Windscreens, f****** tea cup. Just anything to get beyond the first round for a change.

Colin reckoned there was a weak mentality at the football club. For whatever reason, when it came to cup ties we just couldn't seem to hack it. It wasn't as if we got beaten by any good teams. Accrington Stanley did us at Valley Parade, Darlington as well – I wouldn't mind so much if the other team could actually play a bit. But we'd beat ourselves.

So going to Rochdale that night, Colin made it clear that he wouldn't accept yet another failure. Their manager Steve Parkin had them all fired up for the game and you could see the fans thinking here we go again. But it didn't turn out like that. I'd scored a hat-trick in 25 minutes and we pissed it 5-0. Everybody wondered what all the fuss had been about.

I had already got six goals in the first seven games. Here we go again. At this rate, I'd be reaching my prediction of 15 before the clocks went back. I was flying. But I still never expected a Premiership club to come in for me.

We'd finished training the morning after the game and the lads fancied a pint in the pub up the road from the ground. My mobile rang and seeing that it was Julian Rhodes, I walked into the car park to take the call. Just as well I did because nobody would have believed what he was telling me. Paul Jewell wanted to sign me for Wigan!

F****** hell, here I was at 36-years-old and he believed I was good enough to play in the Premiership again. I could barely catch my breath. I've known Jagger a long time since he first signed me for Bradford. We live quite near each other and have become good friends over the years.

I remember coming back from holiday soon after signing for Middlesbrough and there were these little posters plastered over all the windows of the house with the words "Jewell Towers". He just wanted to remind me that if it wasn't for him buying me from Oxford, I wouldn't have had that big home!

Being an ex-Bradford City manager, Paul would still come and watch home games when he could so he knew all about me. He could see I was scoring goals and was still fit enough to play a major role.

Having got Wigan up, Paul was struggling to attract strikers. Most people he was after turned their noses up because the club's name wasn't big enough – that's the problem when you've just got promoted. Everyone expected them to go straight back down. Still, the last thing I expected was for Paul to put in a bid for me. But there was Julian on the other end of the phone saying that Wigan had offered £350,000 with another £150,000 at the end of the season providing they survived. That's £500,000 for a 36-year-old striker playing in League One ...

I didn't know what to think. Of course I was tempted. They were only offering me a contract for the rest of the season at first. But the money was fantastic - £8,000 a week plus another £2,000 on top for appearances.

It was obviously a hell of a lot more than I was on at Bradford. But funny as it sounds, the money wasn't everything. I had to decide whether I wanted to carry on playing regularly for Bradford or being a bit-part player with a Premiership side. There were no guarantees I would walk straight into the side and could I put up with being on the bench every week just waiting for the odd ten minutes here and there?

I'd had that at Middlesbrough a few years before. And I'm not being funny but I'm hardly the type of player who can come on as a sub and change the game straight away. It takes me ten minutes or so to get going and by that time the referee has blown his whistle and the game's over. I wasn't any good as a sub when I was younger. You never saw me come straight on and ghost past four or five players so I was hardly likely to suddenly start doing that at my age.

If I hadn't played in the Premiership before then it might have been different. I would have bitten Wigan's hands off. But there was a lot more to it than that. It wasn't about the fame or the money; I just wanted to play football.

I still had two years left on my Bradford contract and with Helen just starting in the police force, we didn't need the upheaval of me starting at a new club.

The family life was great because I could take the boys to school in the morning and be there to pick them up at the end of the day while the missus was working. That would have all gone out the window if I'd have to drive to Wigan and back every day. And if I didn't get in the team, did I want to be slogging over there all the time and just turning out for Wigan reserves? So I said no.

It was the biggest decision of my life and Helen had left it up to me to choose. But I knew I'd done the right thing.

Jagger sulked for a few weeks afterwards. I don't think he could believe that I'd turn it down. There were no hard feelings but I went to a barbeque at his house soon after and his missus said that I must have been mad.

Julian was made up about it and Bradford improved my contract, which was nice of them. I know there was a bit of talk going round afterwards that this had been some kind of scam dreamt up by the Menston mafia – me, Jagger and John Hendrie – to get me a better deal but that's crap. Julian had the fax from Wigan to prove it.

I wonder if Julian felt quite so pleased at the end of the season when Wigan stayed in the Premier League – I'd cost him £500,000. But I just got on with it and there were no thoughts of "if only" from me. I was playing week in, week out, scoring goals and enjoying my football. And I genuinely felt that I could get promotion back to the Championship as a Bradford City player.

I don't think there was a stranger transfer story than that all season. Nobody would have seen that coming – I was more surprised than anyone. And, who knows, if I had been five years younger then my answer might have been different. But you can never look back in life. Something happens and you move on. You make a decision and stick with it. There were no regrets on my part at saying no.

There is no substitute for playing. All the money in the world means nothing if you can't do that. I hate missing any game so to spend every week sat there on your arse waiting for someone to get injured or play crap wasn't for me.

Bradford rewarded me with a very good package and I like to think I paid them back by banging in another 20 goals that season. Unfortunately the promotion part of the deal didn't come off, though, and we finished mid-table once again. We weren't quite good enough but the season wasn't all bad. And it was great to play alongside someone who was actually older than me!

I was delighted the day Steve Claridge walked into the dressing room. There he was pushing 40 and I felt like a youth-team player next to him. Colin signed him at the start of the season to bring in a bit more experience. I think we were about his 40th different club and his kit bag must have contained gear from every single one of them.

You'd look at him in training and he'd be wearing a shirt from Millwall, Cambridge shorts and Birmingham socks. He wouldn't wear the same outfit twice!

The gaffer used to get pissed off and tried to fine him for turning up in kit belonging to other clubs but he gave up after a while because there was so much of it. But he's the fittest lad I've ever worked with.

We'd take the piss out of him and he was a really funny character but he was so dedicated to the job. He had to be to still be playing for that long.

The banter was always flying when Steve was around. He was the southern bastard and I was the northern monkey and we'd always have a go about the way we talked. He always used to get nutmegged in training when we played circles and would hate it. But could he run!

Steve wasn't quick as such but he could just keep on going. Colin let him take the warm-ups one day so we had a minute walking, a minute running and then a minute sprinting as quick as you can. I was always at the front anyway so I had no worries about the silly old bastard. I'd beat him easy.

We started walking, then went to jogging before Steve shouted go – and I've never seen anyone run like that in my life. It was like f****** Steve Cram. I tried keeping up with him but there was no chance. He just kept on going and going until the minute was up and he shouted stop. I was about 70 yards behind him!

He was 39, I was 36 so you can imagine what the other lads must have been thinking. They were 21 or 22 and all of them are 500 yards behind us. We did six of those runs and it never changed. He kept up the same pace when it came to the quick bit – the rest were miles behind. Afterwards I wanted to know one thing. Steve, why don't you f****** run like that on a football pitch!

You'd seen him in a game and he looked like a Sunday League player with his socks down his ankles and shin pads hanging out. He'd come in the changing room and get his boots out the bag and they'd still be muddy from the week before – he would never clean them. One boot would be a different make to the other so he looked a right mess. But maybe it got him a few extra bob from the sponsors having two companies on his feet.

He was also doing a lot of TV and radio work while still playing for us. We'd be in a hotel before an away game on the Friday night and there was Steve 200 miles away on the telly with his headphones on! I'd sit there thinking that there's no way he can be resting and getting prepared properly but the next day he'd come out again fresh as owt and giving it everything.

He was just a naturally fit lad. He did the right things and looked after himself which is why he was able to keep playing for so long. As everyone knows, he likes a bet and got me into gambling – the bastard. Ring him up and he'd cover your bet on anything. I got on really well with him and he was great round the dressing room at that time. You could see that all the younger lads looked up to him. He was a real eye-opener.

Nobody had a problem because he didn't train with us all week because you knew how fit he was. Colin brought him in for his experience and that helped. He'd been there, seen it, done it and scored a lot of goals in his career, including in the top flight when he was younger.

But Steve probably didn't start as many games for Bradford as he would have liked. He was coming up from the south all the time and you could understand him getting a bit pissed off when he was on the bench.

We caused problems when we played together because, at our age, we both knew where the goal was. Neither of us could bomb beyond defenders but we could read the game a lot better than the youngsters. He would come short and I'd pull off because I was the younger one and it was a decent partnership while it lasted.

RED CARDS AND DEATH THREATS

I'VE BEEN SENT OFF IN SOME DAFT WAYS in my time. Three red cards in one for Aberdeen takes some beating and there was that trouble with Joe Ross at Luton winding me up about the score after the game.

But I bet you've never heard about a player being sent off in the car park before! That's what happened to me with a referee called Darren Drysdale after Bradford had played Brentford.

It had been a really good game, finishing 3-3, and he awarded us a pretty soft penalty right near the end. But he'd given me personally f*** all, no fouls, nothing. We'd had a bit of banter flying around about it. I was having a go at his bald head and he'd turn round and say that I reminded him of Gazza because I was fat – but didn't have his talent.

I didn't think there was anything in it. It was just the two of us throwing the odd comment at each other and I didn't see a problem. He didn't book me so I can't have been that out of order. I went upstairs afterwards for a pint with the family and my little boy Jordan wanted to come home with me. Helen and Josh went off in her car leaving the two of us.

We were just pulling out of the car park when I saw Drysdale and three other blokes coming out of the main door. I presumed the other two were his linesmen and the fourth official, although I suppose it could have been the referee's assessor. He spotted me and gave this silly wave with his fingers bent, like he was taking the piss.

I wound the passenger window down and leaned across Jordan to have a go back. "Don't give up your day job, you prick," I shouted as he carried on giving this stupid little wave. Even Jordan joined in. "Yeah, you duck egg," he said quite loudly – I think that's what got me the ban!

Drysdale didn't say anything back and I thought nothing more of it. It was the sort of banter you hear on a football pitch every week and not worth getting upset about. People say things all the time after games and you just shrug it off. It's not personal or anything like that.

The first I knew about it was later that night when Jon Pollard, the Bradford secretary, rang me to say that he'd received a complaint from the referee. I wasn't worried. Nowt was going to happen because it was no more than a bit of banter. I'm sure the FA have got more important issues to worry about ...

Colin Todd asked me about it at training but I wasn't expecting anything more than a little tap on the knuckles. Yes sir, no sir, sorry sir, won't do it again, that sort of stuff. But then the bombshell letter arrived at the club. I was guilty of bringing the game into disrepute and was going to be suspended. For five f****** games! I was totally gobsmacked. It seemed a completely over-the-top punishment for something and nothing.

I might as well have got out the car and smacked him if I'd known the ban was going to be that long. At least then the suspension would have seemed justified. But this was crazy and I couldn't do anything about it. It was pathetic that a grown man had gone telling tales to his bosses and I was carrying the can for it. Let's not forget that he'd been dishing it out during the game just as much as me. But of course

I couldn't prove that. I could have argued the charge and appealed to the FA but it would have been a waste of time and money.

As far as they were concerned I'd been guilty of effing and blinding at the referee in the car park and had to be punished. They had the perfect excuse to make an example out of me with this nonsense suspension.

It was only recently that they'd changed the rules giving referees the power to still be able to punish players so long after the game like that. Once again, though, it was easy to blame the player. Wouldn't it be nice if just once in a while the officials took a look in the mirror and thought about their own actions.

Jon Pollard told me to take it on the chin and he was right. With three witnesses alongside him, Drysdale was not going to change his mind. If he'd been on his own, he'd have probably laughed it off or said something back tongue-in-cheek. Perhaps with the others there, he had to show who was boss.

It was massively frustrating for me because it meant I missed a month of football. I'd train constantly, doing two sessions a day, but there was nothing to show for it at the end of the week. Just this empty feeling that however hard I'd been putting it in on the training ground, I still wasn't going to be involved in the match.

You play football to look forward to the weekend and the best I could do was join in with a bit of commentary for the local radio. Unlike some players, I don't mind watching games and it helped me to feel a small part of it still.

I'd go into the changing room before kick-off to gee the lads up and then I'd be sat in the stand like any supporter wanting them to win. And when Bradford were away, I'd still take in a game at my local non-league club Guiseley – anything just to be able to watch some football. But I did feel guilty for Colin because I'd let him down. Here was his top goalscorer stuck in the stand because I couldn't keep my mouth shut. However hard I trained, and I was working overtime during that period, I obviously felt I owed him big time.

The ban was due to end on April 1, my birthday. When you get to my age, most people try to forget their birthday but clearly I couldn't wait for it to come.

I was excited about being 37 because I knew it mean I could play football again. It was even better because we were at home to Scunthorpe, which meant playing against Peter Beagrie.

Some people wondered if Colin would play me from the start because I'd been out for so long. But Colin knew that I'd been training like a Trojan and how pumped up I would be. And I wanted to pay him back for what had gone on.

Beags had been winding me up before the game. We'd done a TV show together on the Thursday night and he kept texting me through the week.

We got a free-kick early on and I took it quickly and buried the ball in the bottom corner. My first game back and I'd scored in less than ten minutes!

But Beags, being Beags, wasn't going to let me have it all my own way. They got a penalty almost straight after and he put it away. He ran past me celebrating and I tried to wind him up by saying I'd had £50 on him to score first goal. I hadn't of course.

But it was a great game to play in and it went like a dream for me. We won 4-2 – and I came back with a hat-trick. That shut the critics up. People had been slagging me off and calling me a liability to the team. They wanted rid and said I was more trouble than I was worth because of my big mouth.

I probably do open my gob too often but when anybody criticises me I always bounce back. To come back after five weeks and score a hat-trick was the perfect way to stick two fingers up.

Getting slagged off is hardly new to me. You need a thick skin to be a footballer – I should be like a f****** rhino now. So many people have slagged me off through my career but it just spurs you on. And, as I've always said, the day you stop getting slagged off is the day you stop doing your job right. That's when they don't notice your contribution or see you as a threat.

Enough supporters from other clubs have bought me a pint over the years and said they wished I'd played for their team. They might call me all the names under the sun for 90 minutes but they wouldn't mind me up front for them.

I think it's got worse with the internet and radio phone-ins because any idiot can have their say. It makes it very difficult for players because you cannot react. What makes me laugh is that the local pundit on the terraces calling you a useless fat bastard is probably 17 stone and hasn't kicked a ball in his life. It's not as though he's a good-looking skinny lad having a pop – it's an even fatter uglier bastard who's doing it. I've watched these lads who slag you off when they're trying to play on a park pitch. They can hardly stand up never mind kick a ball properly and they are criticising us!

But I do listen to radio shows and fans forums because I'm intrigued to know what people think. Supporters pay money to go to football and criticise; they work Monday to Friday to earn enough to slag you off on a Saturday afternoon. I'm interested in what people say or write about you. But they pay good money to have a moan and criticise so I'd never have a go back.

I might do something tongue-in-cheek like lifting my shirt up or giving the crowd a stupid smile but I'd never go further than that. Sometimes you get upset with people but you have to bite your tongue – you see what happened when Cantona lost it. I try to put a bit of humour into the game because that's what it needs. Football is a serious business but that doesn't mean you can't have a laugh and joke at times. It's a sport and you do sport because you enjoy it. Just because you might do the odd silly gesture, it doesn't mean you aren't trying to win the game just as hard as everyone else.

But sometimes people cross the line. Shouting and swearing at you is one thing but nobody deserves to receive death threats. I'm not talking about the "Windass, you wanker" type hate mail or rubbish like that. The stuff I received last year was far more chilling – especially when it is delivered to your own front door.

When you pick up hand-written notes on your doorstep warning that next time you walk into Bradford, you will be dead. That's way beyond people having a pop. I'd had it once before when I went up to Aberdeen. There were a couple of letters having a go at the English bastard and telling me to watch my step when I'd got sent off. But it just sounded like a couple of nutters so I ignored it and that soon stopped.

What happened after I'd got sent off against Bournemouth last season, with it being much closer to home was genuinely worrying. That's when you fear that something might happen to your family – and over what?

All right I'd done something stupid on the pitch. I got sent off for a foul on Bournemouth defender Neil Young. I wasn't proud of it; it was a late and nasty tackle and I deserved to go. But does that justify some warped sicko trying to have a go at me and my family? The red card was my own fault. I was trying to prove that Dean Windass had not gone soft in his old age.

A few weeks before that game, I'd started to wonder if I was still putting myself about enough. Defenders were forgetting that I was around and I was not being as physical as I should be. I had a little reality check. I didn't want people thinking that Deano had lost that edge that got me through my career. I wasn't doing it deliberately but it felt like I was operating in a bit of a comfort zone and I needed to snap out of it. That aggression and playing on the border line is what my game has always been about and something was missing. I needed to make my mark again.

I went on the radio the day before the game and told the fans that

I had to get that aggression back if I was going to start scoring goals again. No more Mr Nice Guy.

I was going to stamp my authority on the Bournemouth game. Unfortunately I did that all right, right on Young's leg after about ten minutes.

He had already elbowed me from behind early on. I saw him coming and he caught me on the back of the head. It was the latest in a line of smashes I'd been getting off defenders in previous weeks and I'd had enough. It was time to let him know I'm there. The ball popped up and was there to be won – I swear I didn't go to break his leg. I would never do that. I went on top of the ball but it was an horrendous tackle. I won't deny that. I knew at the time what I'd done and it was a mistake. Everybody makes them.

Their players all came running across but I would have done the same if someone had done that to my team. I was out of order and had to go. I wasn't proud of what I'd done and tried to apologise to the lad after the game. I knocked on their dressing-room door and walked into the middle of their players and went to shake his hand. I had been massively out of order and I wanted to say sorry. But he was having none of it.

He said he'd lost all respect he'd had for me and wouldn't accept my apology. Fair dos, if I'd been on the receiving end like that then I'd have probably wanted to twat me instead of shaking hands.

But I thought that was the end of it. Of course I was in trouble because there was another three-game ban on the way for a straight red and I'd be fined by the club. But I didn't think it would ever get as personal as it did.

The team had gone off the boil and the crowd were getting angry. We'd started the season so well but the wheels had come off for a couple of months and they were looking for someone to blame. We were having a few problems with the fans in previous games and were getting booed at half-time even if we were coming off at 0-0. It was frustrating and some of the younger Bradford players couldn't handle that week in, week out.

It's at times like that when a team looks to their older heads to be able to calm the situation and I hadn't felt I'd been doing my bit. Then to get sent off like that made everything ten times worse. The fans hammered Colin Todd that day even though the lads hung on with ten men to get a point. And I got a bit of stick in the papers for the next few days.

Fair enough, it was a bad tackle but I hadn't killed anybody and I was sure it would quickly blow over if I kept my head down. I made a public apology to the manager, chairman and the fans so what more did they expect? Maybe I should have walked through the city centre with a big white flag saying I'm sorry – would that have made it any better?

All right, I was in the wrong and not for the first time. But life goes on.

The following Friday morning, six days later, there it was. On the doormat, bold as brass. It just said Dean Windass on the envelope. No stamp, no address, nothing else. I opened it innocently, not expecting for a minute what I was about to read.

"If you ever step into Bradford again, we're going to cut your throat. You're a f****** disgrace."

My first reaction was to laugh it off as a joke. Somebody is taking the piss here, though it wasn't very funny. Then I started to think that perhaps it was for real. I should have told Helen straight away but I didn't want her to know. She's a policewoman and I didn't want to make a mountain out of a molehill. If she took it in to work, the whole situation would get blown up out of all proportion and after all it was probably just one sad bastard.

I ripped the letter up and threw it in the bin. Then three days later I got another one. Again it was written by hand, although I couldn't tell if it was from the same guy. I'm not that intelligent to study it that closely. But it didn't look like the same writing. And the words were different.

"F*** off out this football club, you big-time c***."

This was now getting serious. One nutter's abuse you can accept but when two letters turn up at your house like that within a matter of days, then you've got to wonder what they are going to do next. When a third one arrived – "You come into Bradford and we'll kill you" – I had to tell my wife. But even then I ripped them all up and left it a week before letting her know what had been happening.

I shouldn't have waited like that. Looking back now, it wasn't fair and I should have said something to her sooner. These nutters knew where I lived so what if something had happened to the kids or my wife? I would never be able to forgive myself.

Helen told her sergeant and we had a panic alarm system fitted in the house just in case. But we were all jumpy about it.

I was hoovering the car in a petrol station the day after the third threat had arrived. This motorbike drove in behind me and the guy in the helmet riding it just seemed to be stood there looking at me. Next minute, I sensed he was right behind me and I thought 'this was it' so I jumped in the car and locked it! As I did that, he walked past and over to the cashpoint. He was just taking some money out! I felt a right daft bastard but it shows how wary I'd become.

But sadly that's the world we live in. You get these nutters who will say these threats and some who even carry it out. Look at what happened to Ronnie Wallwork at West Brom. I played at Bradford with him and he's the quietest man in the world. But he ended up getting stabbed by some bloke in a bar.

This was only about a month later so you never know what's going to be round the corner. You know it's just a minority trying to frighten you and you shove it to the back of your mind, but that fear is still there. Though as my dad used to tell me, if somebody's going to do anything, they won't tell you first.

But it was disappointing that after all I'd done for Bradford City, there were people out there who were doing this to me. I know it's not all the supporters – they might not even have been Bradford fans – but it still left a horrible taste.

LOCAL HERO

THERE HAD BEEN SO MANY RUMOURS down the years about me going back to Hull. Every time that they went a few games without scoring, you could guarantee my name would be linked. If I got spotted out having a pint with my dad or shopping anywhere round the city, then it must mean I was about to sign for the Tigers again.

It was the same every transfer window and most people just treated it as nothing more than a silly story in the papers. Once or twice there had been a chance that something might happen but I never really expected it. As I said, it was just daft paper talk. So you could imagine the shock I got when the Bradford chairman Julian Rhodes called to say that he was after a big favour.

"I need some money quickly to pay the wages," he said, "and I thought maybe you could go out on loan for the rest of the season to help. There are a couple of clubs interested, Sunderland and Hull."

Hull? Get in there! I jumped at the offer.

I wasn't looking to get out of Bradford, though it had been a bit tough since the Bournemouth red card, but this was my dream to go back and play for my home club again. Sunderland were going well under Roy Keane but as soon as Julian mentioned Hull, there was only one place I wanted to go. I got a text from the Hull boss Phil Brown asking if I wanted to play behind the front two because the wee man Nicky Barmby was injured. Once I got that, I was away.

Everything was kept quiet for a few days until the move was confirmed. I was in the pub across the road from Bradford's training ground having a pint with Richard Edghill when Julian rang again to say that the deal was on. I couldn't get over to Hull quick enough!

It's ironic that it took Nicky's injury to get me there. We're both Hull lads and have known each other since we were kids. People always used to say that we couldn't play in the same team because we were too similar. Now he'd done his ankle and while I felt sorry for him about that, it had opened the door for me.

The fee was sorted out and everybody was happy. The Bradford lads may not have realised it at the time but they might not have got paid in January or February if it hadn't happened.

Once again, the pressure was on. Here I was coming up to 38 and still expected to prove myself good enough for this latest challenge.

Hull were in big trouble in the relegation battle at the bottom of the Championship. There were quite a few teams down there, including Leeds, and nobody could afford to cock up. Don't worry about it, I told Browny, on my first day at the club. If it goes right to the last day of the season, I'll take it. There's no way I will let Hull City go down.

Big words, as usual, and some must have been thinking that he'd opened his big gob again. But I really felt, deep down, that we would get out of it. I must have been off my head! I'd got 12 goals with Bradford and I said to the Hull goalkeeper Boaz Myhill that if I got eight more to take me to 20 then we'd definitely stay up. I only wish I'd predicted my lottery numbers the same day!

My dad and mates were made up that I was going back to the Tigers and it was big news in Hull. The papers were full of stories about the returning hero and all that bollocks. But it all meant that I had to come back and perform. Everybody seemed to remember what I'd done in my first time at the club up to 1995 – now it was 12 years later and they were expecting me to carry on from exactly where I'd left off by scoring goals. I wasn't going back to toss it off.

That first day driving into Hull was very emotional for me. It was like I'd never been away. As well as the change of stadium, the club also had a different training ground from before although it was hardly that new to me. It was where I used to play cup finals back in my days with Northwood against the likes of Swanfield so I knew that pitch very well.

And people like Freddy Cowell were still knocking around the place. He was a scout there when I was 13 and was still walking around the building. It felt very strange. I have to admit I got a bit choked putting on the training gear and looking down at the Tiger badge. It was like being a kid all over again and watching my heroes at Boothferry.

I'd only been back at the club for a couple of days when Browny took us away for a few days in Portugal. It was an international weekend so there was bugger all else to do with no league games and he thought it would be a good idea to give us a break from the pressure of fighting relegation. It was a great chance for me to get to know all the lads, though I bet they felt the manager had signed a right one here when I got totally bladdered on our first night.

I was hardly the new "boy" at my age because I was the oldest by quite a long way. Nicky Forster was next and he was 33. Some of the younger lads took the piss and Boaz asked me if my legs would be up to playing twice a week because I was such an old f*****. I soon put him in his place, the cheeky bastard.

But Browny knew I had the experience of playing under pressure. I'd had a few relegation battles in my times and only gone down once before. I had no intention of that happening again, especially with my home-town club.

Portugal was a great laugh. We did some training, played some golf and drank plenty of beer. But everyone got on and you could see how relaxed we were.

Not that the results came straight away. I had to wait for my chance because big Jon Parkin was playing up front and when I did get my first start, it was out of position. But I won't forget that first game at the KC against Leeds. With so much resting on it, there were nearly 25,000 people there on a Tuesday night and the atmosphere was electric. It had cost me a fortune because I must have bought about 25 tickets for family and friends.

It felt brilliant running out knowing that they were all there and the reception I got from the Hull fans was unbelievable. I'll never forget that as long as I live. Unfortunately the result went against us and I didn't play too well. But after a little while, it came good in the end.

The tide turned for me against Birmingham, who were pushing hard for promotion. I'd been in the gaffer's ear solidly about playing down the middle and promising him goals if he played me there. He must have had enough of me going on about it because finally I got the chance to start at centre forward that afternoon.

It was another massive match in front of a 20,000 home crowd and I was desperate to get off the mark. Then good old Ray Parlour whipped over a perfect cross and all I had to do was tap it in. We got a penalty in the second half and I made it two and really should have finished the day with a hat-trick. But we'd won and I'd scored both goals in front of the Hull fans.

It was a great feeling though I have to admit it still wasn't the same as Boothferry Park. For me, that will always be the ground that I think of with Hull. I know the KC is a superb stadium and the atmosphere is great but I grew up with Boothferry. I still drive past it now and get a lump in my throat. Not that it's a football ground any more, just old fields and long grass waiting to have houses built on it. But I can still picture it in my head.

I was lucky enough to go back a couple of times with Aberdeen and Middlesbrough to play pre-season friendlies which was brilliant. But every trip past what's left now brings back memories of my apprentice days, whether it's sweeping the terraces or shoving my hands down the bogs to clean them. It sounds horrible now but looking back, they were great days.

The situation at the bottom of the table changed round every week. Every side seemed to go on a little run and then drop back just when you thought they were out of danger. There must have been six or seven clubs caught up in it and nobody could hold their nerve to pull right clear.

Southend, one of the teams down there, came to the KC the day before my birthday. Once again it was a six-pointer that nobody could afford to lose. Luckily it was one of those games where everything went right for me. And like the year before when Bradford had beaten Scunthorpe I picked up an extra birthday present – the match ball after scoring another hat-trick.

I've scored a few down the years but this was the best feeling in the world because it was Hull. The last time I'd got a hat-trick with the Tigers must have been at Boothferry against Barnet!

We were all over Southend and once I'd got two, I knew there was a great chance of completing the set.

Andy Dawson crossed it to the far post and I had my hand up like Pele in Escape to Victory when he's waiting for the ball from Bobby Moore. All right, he did an overhead kick and mine wasn't quite as good as that. But Daws picked me out brilliantly and all I had to concentrate on was hitting the target. It was a volley in the bottom corner.

The momentum from that win should have been the springboard to get us well clear of the bottom three. But just like everyone else, we'd follow up a couple of wins with a dip. With two games to go, it was still too close to call between us and Leeds to see which of us would hang on.

They were at home to Ipswich and we were at Cardiff. But the good news for us was that Cardiff had blown their chances of getting in the play-offs the week before and didn't have owt to play for. And I don't care what anyone says. At that stage of the season if you've nothing to aim at, then it's very difficult to raise yourself. But we still knew they wouldn't be rolling over. We had to do a professional job at Ninian Park and keep the pressure on Leeds.

The build-up was very tense and a lot of our fans had gone down to Wales. We were desperate to come away with something but the mood was good after we'd got a big point at Stoke in our last away game.

We'd played really well that day and thrown the kitchen sink at them after going a goal down. But it looked like we'd end up with nothing until Nicky Barmby, who was fit again, hit a last-minute equaliser. It was a huge goal because it kept us out the bottom three and every result went for us that day. And it gave us the confidence to do the same at Ninian Park.

It was a really hot afternoon and there was not a lot between the sides. Then Stephen McPhee volleyed at their keeper, he parried and I was in the right place at the right time. I don't know how I got my plastic hip round it but I connected brilliantly and the ball flew in the net. I went mad and charged towards our fans right behind the goal – and straight into the arms of my brother-in-law. He was right at the front and just grabbed hold of me and wouldn't let go.

Then everyone found out that Leeds were only drawing. I'd scored the goal that had kept us up! But we still had to wait another 20 minutes before the celebrations could start. There was trouble at Elland Road and the ref had taken the players off with only a few seconds to go. So we had to wait around for their game to re-start before he could blow the final whistle.

It was a strange feeling afterwards. We all had the pumped emotion from winning but people were just standing around on the pitch like statues while they waited for news from Leeds. I grabbed Ian Ashbee and went for a couple of pints in the players' lounge where we watched the TV to see what was happening.

Leeds came back out again and immediately won a corner. Surely they couldn't ruin it for us now? The reporter at the game was describing the action. The ball's been put into the box, now it's been cleared, now it's coming back again. Blow that f****** whistle referee! Then suddenly he did. It was all over. Leeds were down – we'd done it.

The bus back home was the happiest ever. Everyone had worked so hard and we'd stayed in the Championship. Browny reckoned I'd written the script. Well, it made a great ending to my book!

But it wasn't just about me. Without my eight goals, Hull wouldn't have done it but this had been a huge effort by the whole team. We'd all given everything.

It was probably one of the biggest achievements in my career. It was certainly the proudest to be part of such a special moment for Hull City. Little did anyone know that 12 months later it was going to get even better...

THE GAFFER

I'VE ALWAYS BEEN INTRIGUED about coaching and management. Nosy bastard? Maybe, but it's fascinated me since I was a young lad.

Even when I was first starting off as a wide-eyed apprentice at Hull, I always used to wonder what the coaches were talking about and what made them tick. Brian Horton and Dennis Booth seemed so knowledgeable to a daft kid like me and I loved to hear them discussing tactics and everything that goes into a game. So I suppose it was only natural that one day I'd want to have a go myself and follow them into the coaching side. It wasn't a case of simply waking up one morning and thinking I'll have a crack at it.

Coaching has changed a lot over the years and these days you have to get badges to get anywhere. You have to attend the UEFA courses to pass the various certificates. The B badge means you can manage a club in the bottom three divisions; the A badge allows you to be the boss of a Premiership side. There's also a pro licence for managing the England team or working abroad – but I think that can wait a while!

It was easy to get my first foot on the ladder. I rang the FA and they put me down on the list for a B licence course.

I was due to go down with my old team-mate Stuart McCall but two weeks before the course started I did my bloody back in and had to cancel. The courses only took place in the summer obviously so that meant another year's wait before I could start to become Deano the gaffer.

I was playing for Middlesbrough at the time and there were three of us on the ten-day course at Keele University, Paul Ince, Mark Crossley and me. But there were plenty of familiar football faces when we got there including Shaun Goater, Brett Angell and Peter Schmeichel. They turned out to be great characters and we formed a really good bunch, especially when it came to the late-night drinking sessions in the college bar. Being in a university, we all had these poxy little student rooms with a small single bed, a cupboard and a portable TV. There was no room to turn round let alone stay in them.

I remember big Peter getting to his room and letting out a big scream. How the f*** can I live in this shoebox for the next ten days? He then went heading off to find the management to see about an upgrade!

I didn't really know Peter before then but he was a real gentleman. I'd only seen him on the pitch when he looked completely mad, screaming his tits off at Steve Bruce and Gary Pallister in Man United's goal. But he turned out to be a real gentle giant sitting in the bar every night supping his Guinness. He was nothing like the angry fella on the pitch and even his nose didn't seem quite as red!

The routine during the course sounded simple enough. Practical training out on the pitch during the day with the FA coaches and then a couple of hours of written work in the classroom afterwards. But that was the intimidating bit. As anyone will tell you, footballers don't like classrooms. Nobody minded the coaching sessions outside – that wasn't a problem. But as soon as you sat us behind those desks and the coaches started writing on the blackboard then the trouble began. Not many of us learned much when we were at school before so it wasn't going to get any easier just because everyone was that bit older.

Every day, we'd be sat behind those desks from 7pm to 9pm while the two coaches John Peacock and Andy Barlow went through all these instructions. The work was hard and hot.

The weather outside had been boiling and the classroom felt like an oven. We were always moaning about putting on the air conditioning but there wasn't any so we had to make do with throwing open every window. It still didn't make much difference so one night I decided I'd had enough and wanted to make a point. We were all sat there in t-shirts and shorts and while John and Andy had their backs to us, I stripped everything off.

They asked a question and I jumped up from behind my desk to answer it with my hand in the air like a little kid – and my tackle dangling in the fresh air! Everyone in the room was pissing themselves and the coaches didn't mind. You needed to have a sense of humour like that to get through it.

Straight after each session, the lads would all head for the bar. At 9pm you had a pen in your hand but by 9.01 it was a pint – and the first of plenty. Our group liked a beer and we'd stay up pretty late. One time we came stumbling out after being on the piss all night and walked straight into the coaches heading for breakfast! But they weren't bothered as long as we were on the training ground for 9am. And the drinking squad were all there – in body at least, if not in mind.

After surviving the course, we had to do some more practical work later in the season. It was like homework, which was never my favourite thing, and you also had an assessment when Andy came over to watch you take training sessions. I had to do two 20-minute topics with the Bradford City apprentices. It felt a bit nerve-wracking with Andy watching you but I must have done all right because I got the licence.

I'm now doing my training for the A licence which has involved going on a week's course at Aberystwyth in north Wales for the last two summers. It is obviously more intense which is why it's a two-year thing. There were a lot of academy people there as well as David Wetherall from Bradford, Steve Howey, Steve Brown and Mike Whitlow. Again it's hard work but we've got another good group which helps.

Because you are with each other solidly all that time, you become like a family so it helps that everyone gets on. We've got to go back again next year for another ten days before another assessment.

But it's good to see the lads who've taken the courses going into management jobs. Seeing people like Incey doing well at Macclesfield and then getting the MK Dons job gives you the confidence to pass everything. Mind you, I'd like to know when he finished off his licence. After four days with us, he f***** off to Portugal on holiday!

And I can't understand why Schmeichs went through all that hassle. I don't think it makes much difference when you're presenting Match of the Day.

BACK HOME

MY LIFE in football had gone full circle. Twelve years on and I was a Hull City player again. Hull obviously wanted to do a deal because it had gone so well on loan and Bradford were grateful for the transfer fee. In the end, I went for around £150,000 with Bradford getting extra on top for every game I play. Add that to the money they got when I went on loan and it will end up close to the £500,000 that Wigan offered a couple of years earlier.

It was a good deal all round and I was well happy. I had a long time at Bradford but Hull are my home-town team, the club I grew up with. I wasn't looking for a move but I couldn't have seen myself playing League Two with Bradford. No disrespect, but I've never played in the bottom division in my career and I didn't want to start now.

Any footballer will tell you to try and play at the highest level for as long as you possibly can. I showed during my loan that I could still perform in the Championship. And Paul Jewell has always told me that I'm good enough to do a job in the Premier even at my age. Who knows?

Maybe if Bradford had stayed up at the end of that season it might have been different. Stuart McCall, my old captain there, came back as manager and we had a good chat before the move went through. He totally understood my decision and wasn't going to stand in my way.

I was gutted that Bradford went down after I left. When the loan deal was done, they were 12th in League One and the chairman thought it was a fair gamble to take. He told me at the time that he couldn't see them getting in the play-offs or getting relegated.

Unfortunately it didn't turn out like that. I think their biggest mistake was getting rid of Colin Todd three months before the end of the season. The team had been struggling and some of the fans were slagging him off but whatever the reasons, I still believe that if he had stayed on then they would probably have survived.

I left Bradford with mixed feelings. I spent six and a half years there in two spells and scored 87 goals - only two players have beaten that in their history. But there were always people ready to have a pop at me and looking for any excuse to criticise. Whatever some supporters may think of me there, they should look at my record. I've never been a big head but my job was to score goals for Bradford City and I like to think I did that pretty well. There will be some out there who would have been happy to see me go. But who else scored the goals?

Nobody else ever got in double figures. One season, David Wetherall was the second top scorer - a centre half with six! If it wasn't for me, Bradford would have gone down well before they did. Look at my scoring record and it's as good as any. As the saying goes, you don't realise what you've got until it's gone. Maybe now people will look back and remember me as a good player who scored goals. All right, I could be a daft bastard at times and there were things that I do regret but nobody can say that I never gave my all for Bradford City.

But going back to my home club felt right. Having helped them beat the drop, there was nowhere else I wanted to be. It was such a relief for everyone around the KC to have stayed up. Relegation would have had some serious consequences.

Phil Brown might not have got the manager's job and there were others who would have been out the door. People like the goalkeeping coach Mark Prudhoe, the assistant at the time Steve Parkin and our fitness coach Sean Rush must all have been worried about how going down would affect them. I knew Sean from when we were growing up. We were the same age and had lived in the same area. It would have been horrible if he'd suffered because we'd gone down.

Seeing Brian Horton again was a real blast from the past. Phil had made him his new assistant although I didn't know that 'til I bumped into him at East Midlands airport. I was due to meet the new chairman Paul Duffen in the hotel there. It was pretty strange walking in and seeing Brian, the bloke who'd bombed me out all those years ago, sat there.

The new chairman was just like the old one. He is around the same age as Adam Pearson and came across in a very similar way. He couldn't offer me a two-year deal straight out because of the age factor. But if I played so many games then the second year would kick in automatically.

No problem, I thought, I'll prove I can go out there and do the business again. The gaffer was in there and I told them both not to worry. Keeping Hull up had not been my swansong. There was plenty more to come from me yet.

We had to report back on June 30 for the VO2 fitness tests before pre-season began with a week in Bormio in northern Italy. It certainly beat what I was used to at Bradford. I'd trained all summer anyway to come back in good nick so I was pretty slim to start off with. I roomed with Michael Bridges and we both mucked about taking pictures of each other, sending them to the rest of the lads and telling everyone how fit we were.

Altitude training took a bit of getting used to but you could soon feel the difference. We were up at 6am and straight on the mountain bikes for a 45- minute ride in the hills. Then we'd come back to breakfast before starting training properly at 10.30 - the cycling was a killer first thing so I would nip back to bed for a couple of hours in between. The sun was beaming down all the time and the facilities were fantastic. We'd do three or four sessions every day on the training ground as well as some weights in the afternoon.

We also had to do these stop and start "doggy" runs, which were known as championship and premiership. Most of us started on the championship one, which was easier, but there were a few show-offs who went for the longer ones.

Bridgey, Steve McPhee, Ian Ashbee and Dean Marney all jumped straight up to the premiership. F*** that, I'm not doing that too early. But of course as soon as those four went, the sheep followed so we all had to. Phil Brown had been there before with Bolton and done it all with Sam Allardyce. He knew what to expect and the benefits it would bring.

The gaffer was delighted with how the week had gone and took us out to the town square on the final night. We all sank a few beers and he made all the new lads stand up and do a song. Because I was the club's first signing under Paul Duffen, I was straight on my feet and belting out Oh Carol. Bloody good it sounded too - much better than our Aussie Richard Garcia trying to sing Tie My Kangaroo Down! Let's just say Rolf Harris has nothing to worry about. We all really enjoyed ourselves and it was topped off when Steve Parkin did this hilarious dance which had all the lads pissing themselves.

The next day, Phil took us up in the mountains to this picturesque health spa. The views were amazing as we sat in the outdoor jacuzzis, sweating off our hang-overs. This was the life. We'd all caught the sun but not like Brian Horton. He tans quite easily and by now looked blacker than Jay-Jay Okocha! But it had been a great trip and the fitness work we put in that week certainly stood us in good stead.

I played up front with Nicky Barmby every game in pre-season. We didn't have that many options with forwards and it wasn't until the last day of the August transfer window that we brought in Caleb Folan from Wigan to give us a bit more competition. The friendlies went well apart from one total shocker against Winterton, a local non-league team. I missed a penalty, their centre-forward scored a hat-trick and we got beaten badly.

The gaffer went f******* berserk with us afterwards. It was an awful performance and he wasn't going to let us forget it. In fact, he kept reminding us about it right through the season. "Remember Winterton" he would write on the notice board to make sure nobody slipped to that low again. But that was Phil's standards. One unacceptable game was one too many and he made it plain that we could never play that badly again.

Hopes were high going into the first game of the season. Plymouth at home was a great chance to get us off to a flyer. I began exactly where I'd left off at Cardiff by scoring after only six minutes, knocking in the rebound when Nicky hit the post. As a striker, you're always looking to get off the mark for a season as quickly as possible. I was up and flying and surely sending us on the way to three points.

But that's not how it turned out. We let in some bad goals and ended up losing 3-2. A packed house at the KC had turned up expecting a new beginning - instead they trailed home thinking it was going to be more of the same.

We'd taken a sports psychologist to Bormio and he'd given us all a sheet with the names of the other teams we had to play. Against each side, we had to write down the result we'd expect. Your West Broms and Birminghams were obviously going to be tough. But everyone had taken it for granted that we would beat Plymouth. But as it turned out, the Plymouth game was the only time we went in front and got beaten all season.

That became Phil's other team talk. If we scored first, the stats told us we were top of the league for going on and winning. Like everyone, we soon discovered that it was such an unpredictable league. Right through the season you found that everybody could beat anyone else and the positions didn't come into it. String back-to-back wins together and you go shooting up the table. Unfortunately it took us a long while to find any sort of consistency.

In one team meeting, Damien Delaney asked the gaffer if he thought we could get in the play-offs. Forget it, was the reply, because at that time we simply weren't good enough. The top six was out of the question; we were looking more at mid-table.

I was quite happy with my own form and had got seven goals by the end of November. But Phil still left me out at times which I hated. I was always banging on his door demanding to play every game but he was only doing it for my own good.

He knew how difficult it can be playing Saturday, Tuesday, Saturday and didn't want to be relying on me all the time like Bradford had done.

Colin Todd would have still made me play there even if I'd had a broken leg. But playing in the next tier up was a lot different from League One. Because of the pro zone, the gaffer could see how far you had run and some games obviously took more out of you physically than others.

Phil Brown is always looking at the statistics and his whole approach is very modern and technical. To be honest, his methods of coaching are different class. That's what I want to go into so I'm always asking him things and getting him to explain why he has made this decision and that. I'm at the age now where I look into it and want the knowledge. In the past, I would have f***** off home as soon as training was over.

But really I want to come back as Bob Shaw, our chief scout, because he's always in the office with his feet up doing nowt! He'll be in France one weekend then Italy the next; big Bob has certainly got the dream job.

WORST NIGHTMARE

THE NURSE had effectively signed my death warrant. "I'm sorry, Mr Windass, but a little blood clot has shown up in the scan."

This is it, then. My career over. Just like that, I was never going to kick a ball again. It's ironic really. I'd been so fortunate through my career with injuries but now my luck had well and truly run out. Everything had come to an end on a bed in Hull General Infirmary.

I'd done the injury in training. We were playing a little game among ourselves, eight v eight, and as I turned I felt a click in my right knee. I didn't bother too much about it. The brain tells you it's just something minor and I carried on. I trained again the following day and then played against Blackpool at the weekend.

Monday morning was a different story. The knee felt sore and I went to see Simon, the club physio. I remembered doing my cartilage when I first played for Hull. It was a similar pain and he thought I'd nicked it.

That last time I was back after 18 days, this time he thought it would be fine in seven to ten. Miss one game and then I'll be back. I had a minor op and everything went fine. The surgeon came in afterwards and said that considering the number of games I'd played, my knee was like an 18-year-old's. So much for being an old bastard! But me being me, I wanted to get back as quickly as I could. I never listen.

Simon left me at home for a couple of days and it was doing my head in. When I came back in to the club, the knee was still a bit swollen but I didn't want to waste any time.

He put me on the exercise bike and said to take it steady. Being a busy bastard, I started racing like the Tour de France.

I felt a bit of a lump in the back of my knee because I'd overdone it. So I was ordered home for another couple of days rest. But the pain didn't calm down. Instead the knee felt stiffer at the back and my calf had turned solid. I asked my wife to massage it and she said there was a little lump in there. I had the weekend off but my calf was just getting worse. It had gone red and rock solid; it felt like a f******* rugby ball.

I rang Simon on the Sunday afternoon. He told me to wait there and he'd be straight back. Three or four minutes later the phone rang and he told me I had to go to hospital right away. Helen came with me and we had to take the kids out of school to come with us because it was going to take a couple of days. I could hardly walk by now and when I got to hospital, my calf was five centimetres bigger than the other one.

The doctor said I might have a Baker's cyst on the back of my knee. A Baker's what? It was the name for a blood clot that had exploded because I'd pushed it too fast, too soon.

The worst-case scenario was that the clot was still there. I'd be looking at anything from three to six months out of the game. In effect, that wasn't just season over - it was the end of my career.

I was pushed into another room where a woman injected some blood into my stomach. I was shitting myself because I didn't have a clue what was going on. Tell me the truth, I asked her, what the hell is happening?

I was sent off for a scan. If it turned out to be a Baker's cyst, the body would clear itself naturally. But if it was a blood clot, I'd have to inject myself in the stomach for the rest of my life. I couldn't turn over on my stomach because the knee wouldn't bend. They moved me enough to do the scan and that's when I heard the dreaded words: "I think there's a little clot in there ..."

I looked at my wife and we both had tears in our eyes. It had become a nightmare. The woman went off to get a second opinion. Eventually they managed to turn me over properly and look again. This time, the doctor thought it was a Baker's cyst.

Well make your f******* mind up then. I was going out of my head with worry. Is it a clot? Is it a clot? I was asking the question every two seconds. It was like being in the car with your dad and keep asking him if we're there yet. My career was hanging by a thread here and they couldn't decide. Then came the verdict - it was a Baker's cyst after all. The blood had just exploded in the back of my knee from me overdoing it.

My emotions went from one extreme to another. Having braced myself for the news that my career was finished, I was now being told that give it two to three weeks and everything should be all right. Dean Windass was on the way back.

But Simon Maltby had saved my career. If it wasn't for him sending me straight to hospital that day, the problem would have got worse. Then I would have been finished. He didn't tell me until much later but apparently Simon had discussed the injury with the manager and said that I was unlikely to play again. But luckily he'd not told me that. Instead of a week, I'd missed seven games. But it could have been a whole lot worse.

The team had done all right without me. Their form hadn't pulled up any trees but they were still up there and in contention. It was all to play for. We were due to play Colchester at home and I trained the day before. It had gone well and I texted the gaffer with a cheeky message telling him to pencil me in for tomorrow. I already have done, was his reply.

But there was no point in taking any chances. When I woke up the next morning, the calf still felt a bit solid and the club doctor said there was no way I should play in case I ripped something. It put me back a week but I wasn't going to grumble. I'd learned my lesson after what had happened last time.

I trained fully the following week and was picked to be on the bench against Southampton. We were short on the ground with strikers. I'd been out and Caleb Folan was also injured so the gaffer brought in Craig Fagan on loan from Derby to play up front with Fraizer Campbell. He was going to start the game but did his knee ligaments in our last training session.

When I got to the ground, the gaffer pulled me in and said he had a choice to make. He could either play Henrik Pedersen up front with me on the bench or give me an hour and put Henrik out wide. I wasn't going to say no to playing. So he put me in and I lasted an hour - enough to help us well on the way to hammering them 5-0. I never scored but felt very good in myself.

But Fraizer got the first one to keep our bet going. We had £50 between us on who would score the most goals. The injury did for me and he beat me over the league season but if you count the play-offs - and obviously I did - we finished level on 15.

I'd never heard of Fraizer Campbell when he arrived on loan from Man United in October. But you could tell straight away that the lad was a star in the making. He'd not really played for United apart from in the League Cup when they got beat by Coventry at Old Trafford. Alex Ferguson had played a lot of young lads and started shipping them out afterwards because obviously they weren't ready. Fraizer came to us and we went for a team walk on his first day of training.

I always used to say to Boaz Myhill to start walking off if you saw the gaffer heading your way. The manager only wanted to tell you bad news. In the corner of my eye, I saw him coming towards me. Watch out, I thought, there's a custard pie with Dean Windass written on it. I was right. The gaffer wanted to go with pace against the leaders Watford so Fraizer was making his debut up front with Steven McPhee. I was on the bench.

In the Vicarage Road changing room, I was next to Fraizer. We introduced ourselves and then he asked me to pass him something. F******* hell, I told him, you've only been here two minutes and you've already taken my place. Now you want me to fetch you stuff!

We both started laughing and our relationship was great from that moment.

Some lads at clubs like Man United don't know the game because they get lost in the system. But Fraizer was a revelation and quickly went from strength to strength. He hadn't played Championship football before and I expected him to be a bit worried. I was nervous as hell on my debut. But he was just sat there flicking through the programme without a care in the world. The gaffer spotted him and told him to relax and not fret about anything!

Fraizer was up against Danny Shittu, a 6ft 2in man mountain of a centre half, but he wasn't fazed at all. He backed in to him all game and didn't give anything away. But I always judge centre-forwards on goal scoring and you could tell Fraizer had the knack straight away. We played Barnsley at home and I played him in for the first goal which he stuck away before he showed his power to get a second.

Fraizer was no Man United big-shot. He was just a quiet lad from Huddersfield; looking at him on the training ground it was like working with my son Josh. He was half my age and a real baby face. He was a natural and didn't need a lot of coaching. You only had to tell him things once.

The only bit of advice I really passed on was telling him to run the width of the penalty box. He might be quick but let the wingers chase out wide and do the crossing. Just stay in the box. He did my running for me as a lot of lads have done. Colin Todd had adapted my game like that - if I'd worked for a manager who wanted me running down the channels, I'd have packed in five years ago.

But Fraizer never wasted his runs. You get some centre-forwards who might be quick as f*** but have got no brains. They just run willy-nilly down the sides and away from the goal. As I've always said, the goal is in the middle. It never moves so don't go too far away from it. Fraizer took that little bit of advice on board and got his rewards.

I know he's going to get better. In two or three years' time, when he's a top striker in the Premier League, I'll be able to say I've played with that lad. I can see a big future ahead for him.

But Fraizer's laid-back attitude was typical of the squad. There were no big-time Charlies and everyone looked out for each other. We had one bad week at the start of December getting battered against Preston, when I was sub, and then at Southampton. But that was when Phil's coaching experience came out. Instead of moping around wondering if the wheels had come off, he just told us to forget it and look to the next game. That week has gone now, he told us, we can't do anything about it.

And we won the next game and the one after that, starting a run of ten points from a possible twelve over Christmas. One of those was at home to Sheffield Wednesday when we beat them 1-0 thanks to my free-kick. But I'll remember that day for another first in my career.

At Bradford, I used to take the piss out of Ben Muirhead because Colin would bring him on and then take him off again, a sub getting subbed. I never thought it would happen to me. I was on the bench against Wednesday but Fraizer did his hamstring after ten minutes so I went straight on.

The gaffer always said that if he was going to sub me in games he'd point to me and I was to head to the far side of the pitch to waste a few seconds. With five minutes left, I looked across to the touchline and there he was gesturing at me to move across. Shit! The sub was being subbed. It was the first time that had ever happened to me and the lads took the piss for weeks.

The crowds were building up after the new year. The fans shared our belief that something special was taking place. We were knocking on the door of the play-offs for a while. Every Monday morning, we'd come into training and look at the table but just couldn't get into that top six. But when we did, f******* hell we never looked back.

We went to West Brom while I was injured and won 2-1 and the belief rocketed. Every week we stepped on the pitch knowing we could win. What a transformation from twelve months earlier. People talked about the pressure of staying in the play-off race but I'd take that any day compared to scrapping for your lives at the other end of the table.

This was a piece of piss in comparison.

Football is all about confidence and we had it in spades. We felt nobody could stop us.

THE RUN IN

I WAS GUTTED that the gaffer had dropped me. Three games to go, we're pushing for promotion and he'd left me out the side. And at Sheffield United of all places. That was one match I'd really wanted to play in.

"You'll get your opportunity again," he told me in the changing room. "I just want to give you a little breather."

I looked him straight back in the eye and answered: "I tell you now that I'll come back and score the winning goal that will get us up." I don't know why I'd said it; it just came out. Typical Windass shooting his gob off again.

But Phil Brown knew me better than that. "I know you will," he smiled back. "I f******* know you will."

By now we had cemented our place in the top six. Automatic promotion would have been the icing on the cake but we were happy with the play-offs. We all knew the stat. Hull had never been in the top division in 104 years but we weren't getting nervous.

The chairman was very confident and every time you read an interview with him in the papers he was saying that we were going into the Premier League. F******* hell, Mr Chairman, don't put too much pressure on us.

But we were full of self belief. And it helped that the teams around us kept beating each other. You'd come in after drawing a game and find out that all the clubs round you had got beat so you'd not lost any ground. Apart from West Brom, the others all had their little dips. Watford were going backwards after the great start they'd had. They had not recovered from losing Marlon King, their goalscorer, and couldn't seem to buy a win.

The biggest danger looked to be Neil Warnock's Crystal Palace who were timing their run at the right time. They made their mark when they came to the KC - and I had the stitches to prove it thanks to Shaun Derry.

I'm not going to pretend I've been a saint on the football pitch. I've kicked people in the past and made tackles like the Bournemouth one that I'm not proud of. But I would never go out to deliberately hurt anybody. But that afternoon Derry did me.

We'd changed the system to 4-3-3 for that game and I was told to drop on Derry behind the front two. I was playing well at the time and we were getting the ball down and passing. Warnock pulled Derry over and told him he had to stop Dean. The challenge was horrible and I was left with a gaping wound.

I wanted to go back on but the doc wouldn't let me. I needed twenty stitches in my leg and it took him forty-five minutes to finish. My two boys came in the room and were really upset. You could see the bone poking through the wound.

Then Michael Bridges came in, which was brilliant. He knew how lonely that treatment room could be and was also worried about the kids seeing me like that. His support was fantastic. He could have stayed outside and watched the game but he wanted to check that the boys and I were all right.

Afterwards, I went looking for Warnock and put the question to him. Did you tell Derry to do me? Neil said he didn't think it had been that bad. Then he walked away without giving an answer.

I was still fuming the following morning at John Hendrie's house. We were looking at the picture of the tackle in the paper when my mobile rang. Ironically it was Warnock. He was checking if I was all right and promised me he would never tell any of his players to deliberately hurt an opponent.

Neil, I said, I'll take your word for it. But Shaun's done me and every dog has his day.

It left a bad taste in the mouth but at least we'd won the game 2-1. Ian Ashbee sealed it with a header. Just like Nicky Barmby's goal at Stoke a year earlier, it was the turning point for us. That goal and that win convinced everyone we could go all the way.

We'd gone to Watford at the start of the season when they were top of the league and got beat 1-0. They had a game plan like the old Wimbledon with their direct football. They also had Marlon King up front before he left for Wigan. The tactics did well for them at the time but Watford got found out. Their form after Christmas had been shite and they couldn't win at home.

It was the best draw we could have got for the play-offs. And the team who finished third usually went up. Before the first game, all we talked about was making sure we didn't concede. Coming away from Vicarage Road with a 0-0 would be a great result to take back to a full house at the KC Stadium on the Wednesday night. Scraping a 1-0 win would be even better. You could sense the tension in the air. It was an atmosphere you only get in cup-tie occasions like that.

Seeing the flags flying everywhere and all the scarves and balloons reminded me of the FA Cup semi-final with Middlesbrough. It was no normal league match. Ironically, after all the build-up, Aidy Boothroyd had changed their style. Instead of launching the ball all the time, Watford were trying to keep it short and pass it which maybe suited us a bit more.

It was a red-hot lunchtime and the game was waiting to explode. We got a massive let-off early on when their big centre-half Danny Shittu scored from a corner. The ref gave a free-kick for a foul on Boaz, even though he'd done nothing wrong. Then Nicky popped up with his goal after their defence got in a mess. Our luck's in boys, here we go!

That settled us down while Watford's heads started to go. Then Fraizer headed on to the crossbar and the rebound came back to me at an angle. People afterwards said it was a difficult chance but it was one of those instinctive things you do as a striker. I flicked out my head and nodded it back into the empty net. You beaut!

We'd won the away leg 2-0 and done better than anyone could have hoped for. Yet surprisingly the mood in the changing room was pretty low. Despite winning, we felt absolutely gutted that it hadn't been by four or five. Fraizer had missed a one v one, Nathan Doyle hit the bar and we'd had other chances to score.

We should have been out of sight. Now suddenly there were a few doubts that maybe we'd let them off the hook. Perhaps 2-0 wasn't enough. If Watford came storming out the blocks at the KC and scored early doors, then your arse starts to tweak.

The second leg was a party waiting to happen. Only Nicky Barmby had played at the old Wembley before but now we were all just one game away.

I never get nervous about my own performance but I worry about the outcome. You can do something about your own game but you can't dictate what is going to happen overall. First and foremost, I knew we had to hold it for the first 20 to 25 minutes. Watford would throw everything at us and we just had to hold firm.

So what happened? They came out and battered us to bits. Aidy had changed things again. Nathan Ellington was causing us all sorts of problems playing just behind Darius Henderson who was back from suspension. He's a big unit and put them in front after seventeen minutes. F******* hell, surely we can't blow it.

I tried to calm a few of the lads down. But we were all worried. The place had become a morgue - you wouldn't believe that 20,000 people could suddenly go so quiet. In the back of my mind, I could sense that disappointment from losing with Middlesbrough in the FA Cup. This was my one and only shot at going to Wembley. Please don't let this happen to me again.

Then Barms, or should that be David Nugent, headed in the equaliser right on half-time. We gave him a load of stick afterwards about that goal. Richard Garcia had headed it back in and Barms tapped it in on the goalline - just as Nugent had done when he made his England debut. But nobody cared how it had gone in. It was a priceless goal and it killed them.

Watford had given everything for 45 minutes but now they were back to square one. Going in one up at half-time would have been a different story but we knew that was it. The second half was comfortable. Three late goals flattered us a bit but we were always on top.

Nicky hadn't scored since August but had got his fitness back after a bad injury. His football brain made such a difference to us and his experience of playing on the big stage. He was a strong little character and a great professional. You don't play for England so many times if you're not a top player. And, of course, it was the Hull connection again with one of the local lads getting the glory.

The scenes after the final whistle were incredible. It seemed that everyone was on the pitch celebrating. Wemberley, Wemberley; we're the famous Hull City and we're going to Wemberley! Soaking up the celebrations and knowing we were off to Wembley - this was what everybody in Hull had been waiting for.

Even when there were only 3,000 at Boothferry Park in the 1990s, I always said that the club was a sleeping giant. If an investor came in, everything would take off because the city's so big. Here was the proof; loud and proud. We had a great night afterwards and everybody had a few drinks. Then it was time to get back to business.

The following night, we found out it was going to be Bristol City in the final against us. I sat at home and watched their game against

Crystal Palace with Josh and Jordan and was pleased that it wasn't Palace going through. Not because of Shaun Derry, although the kids were glad he lost, but I just felt Palace were the team to avoid.

Neil Warnock had a very good record in the play-offs in the past and Palace had been on the up. No disrespect to Bristol City, who had done fantastically all season, but they didn't have the same experience.

I always remember Paul Ince's words before the Middlesbrough semi-final at Old Trafford. He told me to play the opposition and not the occasion. Don't get caught up in all the atmosphere around you. Looking at Bristol City's team, they didn't have that many big characters who you know would be able to cope with the big occasion like a final.

Lee Trundle is a great player and had done really well after coming up from League One. But could he handle it at Wembley when there is a place in the Premier League at stake? Big Dele Adebola, who I'd played with for a bit at Bradford, has never been a prolific scorer but he can hurt you on his day. But would he do that in such a big game?

For me, there was no comparison between our line-up and theirs. Looking at the names, I'd have rather had our side every time. I know football's not played on paper and there might have been one or two good players you wouldn't mind having. But man for man, I knew we would be stronger than them. We hadn't beaten them in the league, drawing 1-1 at our place and losing 2-1 at Ashton Gate when I was injured. But that counted for nothing now. This was our moment of destiny and you could feel the buzz within the club.

We had the experience with the likes of Brown, Ashbee and Barmby to help the younger lads keep calm. Then again, f******* Fraizer was the most laid-back player in the dressing room! The relationship between him, me and Caleb Folan was brilliant all season. We were the best of friends off the field and always encouraged each other, whoever was picked to play.

Caleb used to come on as sub for me and would score every time! But it never bothered the kid when he wasn't starting the next game. He didn't sulk about being left out.

With all of us, it was always a case of "please go get us a goal" because we were all striving for the one thing. We all get the rewards at the end. That was the unity that we had.

Michael Bridges was another. He sat on the bench even though he wasn't included in the squad. That moment when he came in to the empty changing room to give me a cuddle while I was having stitches done just said it all. That was the bond we had.

We were all one big team and not just the players. The chefs at the ground, the groundsman, Gavin who cleaned the cars, Neil and Billy in charge of the youth team - even Luke the tramp, our prozone man - everyone had their little part to play in our success. So it was no surprise that it all clicked together for 90 glorious minutes.

The biggest problem for me was the gap between the semi-final and final. Eleven days is a long time to be hanging around. The gaffer gave us the first couple of days off to rest but I couldn't just sit around and switch off. I was thinking about Wembley 24-7.

The press were on the phone a lot and when we got back to training, all the coverage seemed to surround me and Nicky Barmby as the local lads and Ian Ashbee, the captain.

It was a very special time for Ash because if we went up, he'd have played for Hull in every division. Jan Molby had brought Ash to the club and I used to wind him up by saying that I had been a better captain and Gareth Roberts before him. But nobody had ever achieved what he was on the brink of doing. No wonder the lad was so proud. I saw his wife Anna when Ash got the goal against Crystal Palace. She was holding their little baby Stan in her arms and crying her eyes out. That's how much it meant to her and the family. I was made up for him.

Ash's best mate Gavin Mahon had won the play-offs with Watford and picked up the trophy at the Millennium when they beat Leeds. Now he was desperate to do the same.

The gaffer tried to keep things as normal as possible. He wanted the build-up to be exactly the same as before the Watford away game. We stayed in the Grove Hotel again, well away from the supporters, ate the same food and had the same team meetings. But it was the right thing to do.

As Colin Todd always used to say to me, the only thing that changes in football is the opposition. It was important to keep some kind of routine and treat the following day as just a normal game. Getting to sleep wasn't easy. I used to get nervous as a young lad the night before games but as I've got older it's not been a problem. But it was impossible not to think about what was at stake. F******* hell, it was so close.

I room with Bryan Hughes and we were mucking about with the ringtones on our phones as we tried to nod off. Bryan had also played in the Premier League before with Birmingham. That was one of the reasons he came in, to give us that experience of playing in the top division.

Like Wayne Brown, Jay-Jay Okocha and Henrik Pedersen, Yozzer was another strong character who wouldn't crumble. Another individual you wouldn't swap with Bristol City.

SATURDAY MAY 24, 2008. 2PM

I'M IN THE warm-up area in our changing room. At Wembley. Our kit man Barry wanders over. I've known him since I was about five or six. We go way, way back.

He just looks at me and stares. "F*** me," he mutters, "we're 90 f******* minutes away. Ninety ... Please, Deano, please."

"I'll try Barry, I'll try."

At that moment it really hammered home what was riding on this game. It was no longer a one-off match against Bristol City; a play-off final. This was what Hull had always been waiting for. This was our date with destiny. Not just the team but the people; every f******* one of them. We couldn't let them down.

Phil Brown had tried to keep us away from the build-up as much as he could. He wanted to keep us focused and not get wrapped up in all the excitement and the noise. That's why we didn't go out on the pitch for a look round before kick-off.

Every game in my football career had always followed the same routine. The players would have a walk about, flick through the programme and have a look at the surface. Phil didn't want us to do that. We already knew what the pitch was going to be like. We'd been on it the afternoon before. We knew it wouldn't have changed other than taken a bit of watering. We knew it needed a stud.

Every lad in that room was itching to get outside and Phil kept us calm, reading our programmes and listening to the music. To this day I don't know if Bristol City did their warm-up outside. We were kept totally away from the outside world. Phil didn't want us sidetracked. So we stayed in for an extra half hour, relaxing and quietly focusing on the 90 minutes that lay ahead.

The changing rooms were massive. When we'd gone down the first time, I felt like a kid moving into a bigger house. But instead of running round to check out the new bedroom, I was looking for my peg and where I'd be getting ready. We were all the same; it was like Christmas Eve. We strolled up the tunnel. F******* hell, the Wembley tunnel. Think of all the great players who have done this. At 39, it was my turn.

Walking out on to the pitch was surreal. Even though the stadium was empty there was a special feel about it. I went round with Steve Parkin to try to find out where our wives and families would be sitting the next day. We tried to make out everything was normal; just the usual build- up. Course it was! All you wanted to do was fast-forward the clock by 24 hours. Let's get this game kicked off.

Now we are there. Sat there; waiting for the nod from the gaffer. Why is the time going so f******* slowly? The bus journey to the ground was a sea of amber of black. Everywhere you looked was a Hull shirt; a Hull flag; a Hull face. Hull on tour. But inside the changing room you heard none of it.

Then we get the nod. Here we go, boys. As we get to the tunnel it is like someone has suddenly turned the volume on full blast. The noise is deafening. There are 36,000 Hull City fans going mental - and I probably know every one of them.

We line up opposite Bristol City on the halfway line to meet the guests of honour. There is the Football League chairman Brian Mawhinney and some bloke from Coca-Cola being introduced to everyone by our skipper Ian Ashbee.

This is what you wish for as a kid. You watch England play and all those cup finals down the years and see all these star names shaking hands. You think that one day it could be you being introduced and singing the national anthem. This is the day; it is me.

All the history of the place and now I'm here with Hull City hoping to get them into the Premier League. I look up for Helen and the kids and give them a big wave. I'm not nervous; I can't wait to f******* start. It's time to crack on with our warm-up.

SATURDAY MAY 24, 2008. 5PM

I'M LAYING FACE DOWN on the Wembley turf. The grass smells good; it smells fantastic. The tears are flooding down my cheeks. I'm bawling like a baby. It's like the taps have been turned on. But am I bothered? Am I f***. I'm in my own little wonderful world. I don't know what to think.

Then somebody taps me. It's a reporter. The media blokes from the TV and radio come running over and want a word. There are microphones everywhere and I just start talking. I don't know what I'm saying. It's probably the same old bollocks but everything is just unreal. Someone is going to pinch me in a minute and I will wake up, realising it's just a dream. Only this is real, very real. Hull City are at Wembley; Hull City are in the Premier League. I'd scored the goal for my home club.

We were just dancing round the pitch; everyone going mental in front of the supporters. Singing, shouting, simply going off our heads. Nobody wanted it to end. This was Roy of the Rovers stuff. No, it was better than that. You couldn't make it up. If somebody had said at the start of the season that Hull would win promotion at

Wembley and I'd score the winning goal, I would have laughed in their face. Don't be so f******* mad.

The final few minutes had lasted a lifetime. I was sat on the bench with Barms with my hands over my eyes. I couldn't watch when Bristol City were attacking but I couldn't look the other way either because of the f******* big screen. So I just sat there with my head down, pleading for Alan Whiley to blow the final whistle. Mark Prudhoe, our goalkeeping coach, lent forward and said there was only one minute to go. What a long minute that was!

Then the whistle went. It was the best sound in the world. I just ran on the pitch and belted towards our supporters. It was probably the quickest I f******* ran all through my career. Linford Christie wouldn't have caught me. We'd done it. We'd f******* done it. We partied on the pitch; we partied in the changing room. But it was only when I reached the players' lounge later that it hit me.

I saw Helen and the boys Josh and Jordan and gave them all a kiss and cuddle. Then I spotted Ian Ashbee sat with his wife in the corner. He was very emotional and as soon as he caught my eye, that set me off. We were both sat there blubbing away. I left Ash and his missus to it and wandered to a table on my own to turn on the mobile. I picked up the phone and scrolled down the messages. They just kept on coming; 99 in all. I sat there and read every one of them.

A supporter came over and asked for an autograph but I asked him to give me five minutes. I wanted to be alone with my pint and my thoughts. And once again the tears were not far away. It was the same sensation as when you have your kids. You want a few minutes to yourself to take it all in and let the emotions go. Helen asked if I was all right. I was fine. But I just wanted that little space to myself to look through the text messages and savour what we had achieved.

The following day we did our open-top bus tour round Hull. No chance of a quiet minute then. Bloody hell, I didn't know so many lived in the city. There were people everywhere you looked. Looking down from the top of the bus, it was just a mass of smiles.

But I still saw a load of familiar faces. There were thousands of people shouting your name but you could still pick out lads from school and those you'd known throughout your life.

We finished up in the square outside City Hall with 50,000 fans cheering. I jumped on the balcony to join in - health and safety must have had a f******* fit. Helen bollocked me about it afterwards but I told her that even if I'd fallen I would have been all right. There were that many people underneath that somebody would have copped me! It was yet another occasion that I will always remember. A special, special day.

But there was still one more celebration to do - back in the local with my mates in the Menston Arms. That meant just as much to me as all those thousands in my home city. I'd got a couple of tickets for Wembley for Alister and Suzanne, who own the pub, and they were as excited about our victory as everybody else. I had to share the moment with them.

So after things had died down in Hull, I went back there with a couple of bottles of champagne. It was a nice way to unwind being with people who will bring you straight back down to earth. No chance of playing the Premier League big shot with that lot taking the piss all the time. We had a few glasses but I was home by 11pm. I was emotionally and physically drained and couldn't handle any more. Not like the rest of the punters who kept on going until 5.30 the next morning! They certainly made the most of it.

As footballers, it's great knowing that we can give a lot of pleasure to a lot of people. In the weeks after Wembley, I realised just how much Hull getting promoted has meant. Even those who weren't really football fans have been caught up in the excitement. Hull is on the map and I feel proud to have been part of the team that has done that.

But you still need to keep things in perspective. The local paper set up a campaign to have a road named after me because of the goal. And they got over 1,000 signatures on the petition. Something like that is very flattering but I don't feel it's right. To hear people calling you a legend makes me uncomfortable.

I'm a footballer and lucky enough to get paid well for what I love doing. But don't say I'm a legend. Legend is a big word and not in the equation for me. In my eyes, legends are people who fight in wars and defend your country. People who put their lives on the line; people who could get killed every day just doing their job; they are the proper legends. And I mean that from the bottom of my heart. It feels fantastic to have achieved something that people in Hull will never forget. But I'm no legend.

They call it the £60m goal because of the amount of money that playing in the Premier League is worth now. And I know that goal will change people's lives financially.

The younger kids at the football ground will get decent bonuses out of it and all the boys behind the scenes. It will also have a knock-on effect for the businessmen in the city because the whole place has taken off. To know you have achieved something like that is pretty special.

But there were eleven heroes at Wembley that day, not just Dean Windass. I got the headlines in the papers but it was a total team effort that got us up. It's like when England won the rugby World Cup and Jonny Wilkinson got all the attention. He knew it was a lot more than just his drop goal that won it.

If it hadn't been for every one of us and what we did throughout the season then none of this would have been possible. There would have been no Wembley. People say it's the best goal scored at the new Wembley and certainly the best in my career. But I would have been proud as punch whoever had got it.

I've never been a selfish person where it's all me, me, me. This was about Hull City and reaching the top division for the first time in their history. All I wanted to do was win the game. I wasn't bothered if I got on the scoresheet as long as I played well for the team and we achieved that. But luckily it was my day - and a momentous one I will never, ever forget.

There was only one slight disappointment. I never got to twenty goals in a season for the seventh time. I said that to the gaffer in my appraisal when everything had died down. If I hadn't suffered the injury and missed those seven games, then I'm sure I would have done it. But I'm not going to complain too much. It still turned out pretty good!

THE MENTOR

BY TERRY DOLAN

I'VE LOST COUNT of the number of players I've signed during my time in management. But signing Dean for Hull first time around ranks as one of my best bits of business. Not to mention one of the quickest.

We knew of this talented lad playing non-league on our doorstep for North Ferriby but we were also well aware that there were other clubs sniffing around. The word on the grapevine said that Sunderland were ready to make a move and there was not a moment to lose.

Bernard Ellison, one of our coaches, watched him in action on the Saturday and came back with another glowing match report. That was good enough for me and we made our move.

By Monday we had Dean in for training with us before Sunderland manager Denis Smith could put in a bid. And I'm glad we did because I knew straight away we'd got ourselves some player.

Dean was a little bit wary of his surroundings at first. But I could understand that because he'd been shown the door by the club once before and must have been worried about lightning striking twice. But we never had any doubts and threw Dean in the deep end by sticking him in with the first team. He was the best player on the pitch and within 20 minutes I knew we had to sign him.

Dean didn't need any persuading and once the contract was there on the table you could see him relax. His confidence had been tempered a bit because this was his second, and probably last, chance to make it as a pro but he signed the forms and was immediately his bubbly self once again.

It's incredible to think that we are talking 15 years since that day and Dean is still playing. And still playing for Hull. So much has happened for him in that time but he shows no signs of slowing down. And why should he?

Of course, I've watched his progress down the years with a lot of pride. I'm also proud that we remain so close. Not a week goes by when Dean isn't on the phone, whether he's asking me for advice on this or that or simply catching up on the latest gossip about who's supposed to be off to where.

Lately, we've been talking a lot about the coaching side of the game as he thinks about what he wants to do when his playing days are finally over. Not that I think he will be packing up for a long while yet. And yes, I can see him becoming a good coach and maybe a manager one day.

He has changed a lot over the years, whatever some people might think. Compared with the character I first signed at Hull, he has mellowed but then he's got a family and two young boys to think about now.

It's his great knowledge of the game that will give him a great chance when he takes his first steps on the coaching side. Here is a player who has experienced all levels of professional football and knows what it's about.

I know Dean's had it in his mind for a few years now that he wants to go into management after playing and I don't think anyone will stop him. When he is set on doing something, he won't be put off. He has been taking all his coaching badges and with his great experience he will be respected in the dressing room. And the one thing that has always stood out for me is his football brain.

Supporters see some of his antics on the pitch and he can act a bit daft at times but Dean is also a very intelligent player. That is why he has kept going for so long; he reminds me in that respect of Teddy Sheringham. All Dean has wanted to do is play football, even during the times when he hasn't been in a club's plans.

I remember when Dean found himself out the picture at Middlesbrough under Steve McClaren for a spell so rather than sulking about it he went on loan to Sheffield United. But that's typical of him, he'd prefer to be playing even if it was at a lower level than just sitting on the bench and not getting involved.

That's probably why he said no to Wigan and the chance to go back to the Premiership a couple of years ago. Again he'd rather be playing week in, week out than just be a member of the squad hoping for a game every now and again.

But you look at his career and he's been a great example for other players. He likes to play the clown but he has always been very fit and takes training seriously, which is why he has been able to go on so long. It's not a coincidence that even though he is approaching 40, Dean is still performing well at a high level and young lads can learn from that.

Dean has also missed very few games through injury - he's sat out more because of suspension! He is a naturally fit lad who doesn't like to be stuck in the treatment room when he can be out there giving his all on the pitch.

As a manager, you can't have enough of that type of player. So it's no surprise that he is still one of the first names on the team sheet.

I was delighted to give him his first chance in professional football and he has certainly grabbed it with both hands down the years. He's a special player and it's been great to be associated with him.

The fact we've kept up our friendship for all this time and still talk on a weekly basis says it all really. I think a lot of Dean and I hope he thinks a lot of me.

THE MISSUS

BY HELEN WINDASS

DEAN WINDASS the footballer and Dean Windass the person are two totally different people. And I should know.

He's a lot softer away from the pitch and doesn't act the hard man that the fans always see. He has always had a little bit of a temper but he never loses it to the extent where he'd carry it out like he sometimes does when he is playing.

I can always tell when he is going to lose it on the pitch. I've watched him in games and know that he's going off – if they don't substitute him, he'll get a red card. You just watch his body language and can see the anger rising up and nobody can do anything about it. When he loses it, it's like the world is on his shoulders. If the game is going badly and he has no control over it, he can get frustrated very easily.

At home, he can lose his temper quite quickly but I wouldn't say viciously. He lets things bother him very easily whereas I can reason with people more. He's got no patience with the kids. Josh will do something that annoys him and he screams his head off instead of talking it through. But, to be fair, when Dean shouts it usually works!

Football is about highs and lows and maybe that's why Dean's personality is like that. He's either very high and full of himself or rock-bottom low – everything is black or white with him and there's no grey area.

He did have a really bad time after being sent off for the two-footed tackle against Bournemouth in his last season at Bradford. Some of the stick he got was asked for but not all of it. Personally I don't think the club should have criticised him in public as they did and that sent Dean into a real depression. They handled it all wrong and Dean didn't take it well.

He's the kind of person who likes to be liked by everyone and when the club came out and had a go, the fans turned on him and that really hurt. Dean knew he'd done wrong with the tackle and deserved to be sent off but what followed afterwards really left him down.

Dean is not one of them who can switch off when he gets home. I wish he would occasionally. But he is always bothered about the result. He's never been one for thinking that he gets paid whatever the score; he always wants to win and score a goal. I wish just occasionally he would shut the front door and leave football outside. But he's like a kid who won't put the ball away. He'll go over and over what happened in a match, especially things like a sending-off. Instead of accepting he's done wrong, dealing with it and trying to move on, he keeps dwelling on it.

The press went to town on him after what happened against Bournemouth, which they do when you do a bad thing. In the same way, they'll praise him when he's scoring goals so you have to take it when it's going crap. You have to take the rough with the smooth but Dean struggles – he can't seem to handle it. He's been like that for as long as I've known him. He finds it hard to cope when things go wrong.

That day he got sent off for the two-footed tackle, I was dreading going home. Josh was so worried that he'd gone down to the changing room while the game was going on to calm Dean down. We didn't know how he was going to react but luckily Dean would never lose it in front of the kids.

But I wouldn't want to go through that time again. Dean was in a real depression and then I found out he'd even been sent a couple of death threats. It's a fine line with that sort of thing. Is it someone just doing it because Dean has pissed them off because they didn't win a game due to him going off or it is a lot more sinister?

It might just be one or two idiots going too far but you have to look at it seriously as a family with two small kids. If these people have taken the effort to find out where we lived and hand-delivered the notes to the house, then you can't be sure what they are prepared to do. I think that takes it to a different level because it is threatening your safety.

He didn't tell me until a while after it had happened otherwise I would have confiscated them and taken them to work – I am a police officer. It was actually a chief inspector in West Yorkshire who had read about it in the press and then got in touch with me. I don't think Dean would have said anything about it because he didn't want to scare me. But we had a chat and he agreed to put an alarm in the house.

I know there were bound to be people who thought he was making it up as some kind of sympathy vote to get the fans back on his side. But it was nothing like that – those letters were genuine. It's a pity I didn't know about them straight off because we would have been able to catch who did it. There are a lot of things the police can do to trace where these sort of letters come from.

I know fans get disappointed and their lives revolve around going to football. But it's the same with Dean – he was hurting, too.

Football is often about that split-second and making that instant decision. And it's not always the right one. I think he suffered for that. Some of the punishment was justified but some was not – and the family don't deserve it either. Fans have got to understand that players are human and they don't mean to make mistakes or do badly on purpose. They don't try to get booked or sent off or play crap just for the fun of it.

Sitting in the crowd, I've learned to ignore most of the comments about Dean. He always gets called a Fat B but that's gone on for so long and it doesn't bother him.

I do sometimes feel like telling people to shut up when they are shouting for him to be taken off saying he's crap and things like that. But he's the only one who's ever going to score, even if he's having a nightmare. No disrespect to the rest of the players, but going on the number of goals he has scored in the last few years that's the truth.

When we first got married and went to Aberdeen, I used to get upset about the stick. I was only 25 sat there with a little baby and being the only English player the fans would shout at Dean, who was an obvious target.

As Josh got older, he used to ask me why people would always shout nasty things about his dad. But now the boys are quite thick-skinned and they've learned to blank it out. You let it just go over your head. Over the years, if someone sat right behind has a go then I have turned round and reminded them that Dean happens to be my husband and these are his two kids. I appreciate you've paid your money but could you just keep it down a bit because that's their dad you are slagging off.

I would never knock fans because football is not cheap, especially if you are taking the family. You do get caught up in the emotion of it because you want your team to win but there has to be a limit. A bit of respect wouldn't go amiss, especially when you've got little ones with you.

The boys never look at Dean as Dean Windass the footballer. It's just their dad playing football and always will be. When he played for Middlesbrough, the Man United team came in the players' lounge and the kids were all over them. They weren't bothered about Dean, their dad, they just wanted all the United autographs.

It makes me laugh when you read about the so-called Wag culture and the footballers' wives and girlfriends. To be honest, I've never been part of that even when we were at Middlesbrough. Up there, they were mainly foreigners so I didn't really mix much. I'd watch the game and then go straight home. Apart from Colin Cooper's wife and Claire Ince, who I didn't see a lot of, there weren't really any other English women.

Moving from Hull to Aberdeen for the very first time had been hard. It was the first time I'd ever left my home town so that came as a big shock. It's the norm and what you're used to and the longest I'd ever been away from Hull was only when I went on holiday.

Dean looked like he was going to Norwich until a couple of days before and I'd got my head round that. Then he suddenly mentioned signing for Aberdeen instead – I didn't even know where it was.

My twin sister Debbie was proper devastated. Mum and Dad didn't want me to go either. Dean found it easier because he's never really had that close family bond and, to be honest, I think the move was the best thing that ever happened to him.

He's always stood on his own two feet but being that far away from home meant he had to deal with everything.

It was very difficult at first until we found a house because we were living in the hotel. But we got used to it. I just joined a running club and it was all right after that. We were married and had a family and you accept that moving around is just part of being in football.

But we've come a long way since I first met him all those years ago. He was playing for North Ferriby at the time and I knew of him because my dad was the manager. Dean was really good friends with my brother but I had a boyfriend and thought he was just a kid who played for my dad.

There was no love at first sight or anything like that. He was talking to me in a club in Hull and just acting like a complete pain in the arse so I quickly got rid of him. But he'd turn up round my mum's and often ask me which one I was, Helen or Debbie, because we look quite alike. Then one night Dean told me he'd left the building site and was going to turn pro. Yeah right, I thought, in your dreams. I asked my dad because he could be a right lying git and he said it was true. In my eyes, Dean was still just a young kid who my dad knew and looked a bit short for a proper footballer.

He was doing a presentation for a team called Beverley Boys and persuaded me to come. I didn't really want to but he said that I had nothing else to do and was stuck at home with mum and dad otherwise – Dean always did have a way with words. We ended up having a really good laugh although that didn't lead to anything straight away because he went off on holiday with his mates. But we kept bumping into each other after that and eventually one thing led to another.

But he used to proper get on my nerves. It wasn't like I fancied him straight away or anything like that.

My family didn't think much of it when we did start going out. They all saw Dean as more of my brother's friend than anything else and wondered what I was doing hanging around with him. My dad was chuffed because he knew him really well from the football but mum wasn't so sure. But they've always just let me get on with it.

I'd like to say that Dean has mellowed over the years and he's grown up a bit. But not a lot.

But in football, when do they grow up? You've got to bear in mind he's one of the old ones compared with most of the rest who are in their 20s. They take the mick out of each other and it's just constant banter so you never really grow up until you're away from it. They are always acting like little boys.

You see players on Soccer AM, diving on each other and messing about, and that's football in general. They are little boys until they leave the pitch and go home.

Dean is definitely a lot quieter at home than how the public see him. But there are probably a lot of things I don't know about that he gets up to. You hear about some of the disgusting things that happen in the changing room but Dean doesn't tell me a lot because he knows I'd be mortified. I bet it's the same at every club because that's the culture when players are together all the time. It's only when they get away from that, then you see the real person again.

Dean loves all the attention that comes with being a footballer. And he would never ever say no to anybody who wants his autograph. Sometimes I wish he could, especially when we're out having a meal or something, but he doesn't want to disappoint people even if they come up to the table while we're still eating.

He gets drunk women coming up to him wanting him to sign this and that. Half the time they haven't got a pen and just want to speak to him but he won't tell anyone to get lost. Dean loves being the centre of attention and enjoys it when people are talking about him. You see that on the pitch when he's clowning about and lifting up his shirt and things like that to wind up the fans.

Some bits are funny but there are times when I just wish he'd stop pissing around and bloody get on with it. He can be an idiot but it does get the crowd going and maybe it lifts himself a bit when things aren't going too well. He always says that when it's noisy the crowd lift you. And, to be fair, at Bradford you can hear a pin drop. There is a big cheer when you score and then it goes dead again.

The banter doesn't bother him because he tends to play better when he gets a bit of stick. Again it's that attention thing which makes him try harder.

Dean has never shied away from anything. If he's not playing, he'll still be sat there in the crowd and he's not one for hiding at home after a bad game. Unlike some players, he's never refused to face the fans. It's just those occasions when everybody gets on his back, he struggles to handle it and his head can go.

But he's got to learn if he wants to go on and become a manager one day. I know that's what he wants though if I'm honest, right now I can't see him doing that. Maybe in a couple of years time things will be different.

Once he's mentally prepared himself that he's not going to be playing any more and got away from the dressing room banter then he will grow up. Then you could see him going into the coaching side. All players act like kids in the dressing room and on the training pitch and like to piss about. When you're a manager you've got responsibilities and you have to grow up fast. You have to stop being a kid and set an example for the squad.

It's going to be a very difficult day when he has to get his head round the fact that he's no longer Dean Windass the footballer. Being away from that lifestyle and banter will be hard because it's all he's been used to. It's not the money or the training, it's the banter and the jokes in the changing room that he will miss the most. And I bet if you ask any footballer reaching the end of their career, they will say the same.

It will be like a big hole in his life.

I think he's got a really good chance of making it as a coach or manager one day. But people need to see the other side of him – the grown-up side. And I don't think you'll see that until he's finished playing.

A WORD
FROM BIG BILLY

BY BILLY WHITEHURST

Big Billy Whitehurst was working as a bricklayer and playing semi-professional football, when he was picked up by Hull City. He went on to become one of the club's most popular players ever. In two spells with the club, 1980-85 and 1988-90 he scored 52 goals in 229 appearances. He is widely regarded as the hardest man to have played the game. Alan Hansen, Neil 'Razor' Rudock and Vinnie Jones have all stated that Billy was the hardest opponent they ever faced. Dean Windass watched Whitehurst from the terraces of Boothferry Park as a young fan and Big Billy was a senior pro at Hull when Dean first arrived as an apprentice. Like Dean, he is still regarded as a hero to Hull fans.

MY FIRST recollection of Deano was when he was about fourteen. It was at Boothferry Park during half-time and these young lads were juggling the balls and doing tricks to entertain the crowd. As I came back on the pitch for the second half, I saw this little lad keeping the ball up and I was just amazed at his ability.

It looked like he could do anything with a football. He was a bit chubby and robust and not all that tall but could he make he ball talk! F******* hell, I said to one of my teammates, I'm supposed to be the professional footballer but I can only keep the ball up four or five times and this kid's doing a hundred. It's a pity a few of the first team didn't have the skill to match.

Deano has never lost that incredible ability. We always go on about the continentals and everyone gets carried away when a Brazilian scores a good goal. But when you talk about technique, Dean has all that. You see the Premier League now and the skill level is getting better but Dean has had that technical ability since he was twelve years old. His touch has never let him down. I've always said the most important thing in football is the first touch because it gives you that time and control to do what you want. Dean has always had that in spades.

He's always been a bit controversial and is certainly a character. But the game needs more of that – players like that are a dying breed. He is never afraid to speak his mind but I bet his is the first name on the team sheet every week. He's not short of an opinion but has the ability to back that up.

You can guarantee that players who are a bit outspoken like that are the ones that get nobbled first by the opposition who want to bring them down a peg or two. Dean expects that and he thrives on it. If he hadn't been such a character, I'm sure he wouldn't have been as effective as he's been throughout his long career. There are not enough like him.

I just wish he had come back to Hull a little earlier. He could have returned two years before and I'm sure it would have happened if Peter Taylor hadn't been there. Some managers want sponges in the dressing room – players who just accept everything the manager says and never question a word. They don't want anybody answering back and questioning their authority. If you profess to be a top manager, you've got to be able to handle the stronger men. Players like Deano who aren't afraid to have their say and tell the gaffer if he's got something wrong.

Last season wasn't all about Dean. Winning promotion like that is a team effort and a lot of players put in a fantastic effort but Deano just added that bit of spark. His performance gave the rest of the players the belief they needed to complete the job.

I went to Wembley and it was such a tight game. There was nothing really between the sides apart from one piece of magic and that was Dean's goal. You won't ever get a better strike than that. It was just perfect. One bit of brilliance saw Hull through and it was a fairy-tale that it came from him.

Would it have been the same ending if that ball had gone back to any other player on the pitch? I'm not so sure but with Deano in the right place at the right time there was never any doubt. You couldn't have written it better. His story had all come together. It was a superb day all-round. Hull's first trip to Wembley in their history and we won to get into the Premier League.

The Bristol City fans were superb afterwards as well and took the defeat on the chin. They knew the result could have gone either way – and if you're going to lose, then it's better to go down to a memorable goal like that.

I've known Dean for many years, since he was an apprentice at Boothferry, and he's never changed. He's a swashbuckling character who always wears his heart on his sleeve. The legs might be getting to the end of their tether as he heads towards forty but the footballing brain is still as sharp as ever and I'm sure there are plenty of games still to come. He's got a couple of strong people in charge of him at Hull in Phil Brown and Nobby Horton who will keep him on the right track.

I know he wants to become a manager and he has got the right attitude. He is a winner. At the end of the day, the manager has to earn the respect of the players to be successful. You only have to look back at his career to see what a great player he has been. If the lads he coaches one day achieve half as much as he has done, then they will have had a very good run.

I wish him well for the future and if Hull is going to give anyone the freedom of the city then it's going to be him. The Hull City people have been on the breadline in the past and they probably can't believe what is happening now. Deano has done so much to achieve that.

Picture Credits:

Jack Harland, Hull Daily Mail: front cover.
Dean Windass' family album: back cover (left), Page 97–101, 151
Hull Daily Mail: 102–108,
Chris Bacon, PA Archive/PA Photos: 109
Matthew Ashton, EMPICS Sport/PA Photos: 110, 145
Mike Egerton, EMPICS Sport/PA Photos: 111
Yorkshire Post Newspapers: 112, 146 (bottom)
Rebecca Naden, PA Archive/PA Photos: 146 (top)
Gareth Copley, PA Archive/PA Photos: 147 (top)
Steve White, EMPICS Sport/PA Photos: 147 (bottom)
Chris Lawton, Yorkshire Post Newspapers 148 (top)
Bruce Rollinson, Yorkshire Post Newspapers: 148 (bottom)
Dan Oxtoby, Yorkshire Post Newspapers: 149 (top)
Gerard Binks, Yorkshire Post Newspapers: 149 (bottom)
Terry Carrott, Yorkshire Post Newspapers: 150
Andrew Brown: back cover (right), 152
Simon Renilson, Hull Daily Mail: 153–158
Kate Woolhouse, Hull Daily Mail: 159 (top)
Darren Casey, Hull Daily Mail: 159 (middle)
Phil Dawes, Hull Daily Mail : 159 (bottom), 160 (top)
Jerome Ellerby, Hull Daily Mail: 160 (middle and bottom)

TRUEMAN'S TALES

'Fiery Fred' – Yorkshire's Cricketing Giant

By John Morgan and David Joy

With contributions from: Dickie Bird, Ian Botham, Geoffrey Boycott, Brian Close, Raymond Illingworth, Bill Pertwee and Harvey Smith.

This book began as a collaboration between Fred Trueman and David Joy in early 2006. Then came Fred's untimely death. Sports journalist, and long-time friend of Fred Trueman, John Morgan, completed the book, which became a fitting tribute to a cricketing legend.

Fully illustrated. Hardback.

BETWEEN THE TIDES

The Perilous Beauty of Morecambe Bay

By Cedric Robinson

Foreword by HRH The Duke of Edinburgh

Cedric Robinson records his 45 years as Queen's Guide to the Sands, an historic role that stretches back many centuries. In this book, Cedric describes the guided walk across Morecambe Bay, the wildlife encountered there and past tragedies on these treacherous sands. Superb colour photographs depict the Bay in all its amazing variety.

Fully illustrated. Hardback.

FROZEN IN TIME

The Years When Britain Shivered

Ian McCaskill and Paul Hudson remember
when winters really were winters.

Using dramatic pictures and news reports from national and regional archives, recalling the worst winters ever with particular attention given to 1947, 1963 and 1979. An exciting and thought provoking read.
Fully illustrated. Hardback.

Visit www.greatnorthernbooks.co.uk

Also by Great Northern Books

SWEET SUMMERS
The Classic Cricket Writing of JM KILBURN
Edited by Duncan Hamilton
(Winner of The William Hill Sports Book Prize 2007)

Capturing a time when the true spirit of cricket existed. Through Kilburn's writing, some of the game's past legends are brought to life among them Donald Bradman, Fred Trueman, Jack Hobbs, Keith Miller, Garfield Sobers, Hedley Verity, Len Hutton and Walter Hammond.

For more than forty summers, J M Kilburn, the Yorkshire Post's cricket writer, captured the spirit and beauty of the game and the legends gracing it, among them Donald Bradman, Fred Trueman, Jack Hobbs, Keith Miller, Garfield Sobers, Hedley Verity and Walter Hammond. He writes of the days when 8,000 people watched Yorkshire's County Championship matches; when he travelled by ship on an Ashes tour with his friend Len Hutton; and of a bygone but beautiful period when one-day matches, coloured clothing and rampant commercialism in cricket simply didn't exist. Now you can explore these summer days in a richly satisfying collection of Kilburn's work gleaned from the *Yorkshire Post*, *Wisden* and *The Cricketer*. Kilburn is worth reading not only because he was a knowledgeable and respected interpreter of cricket – well balanced, tough-minded and scrupulously honest in his verdicts – but also for the valuable historical and social perspective that reading him provides. Most of all he demonstrably cared about cricket. His heart was in it – and belonged to it.
Hardback. Illustrated.

Visit www.greatnorthernbooks.co.uk